◇ The ◇
Oat Bran
Baking Book

The Oat Bran Baking Book

85 Delicious,
Low-Fat, Low-Cholesterol
Recipes

NANCY BAGGETT and RUTH GLICK

CB
CONTEMPORARY
BOOKS
CHICAGO · NEW YORK

Library of Congress Cataloging-in-Publication Data

Baggett, Nancy, 1942–
    The oat bran baking book : 85 delicious, low-fat, low-cholesterol
recipes / Nancy Baggett and Ruth Glick.
        p.   cm.
    Includes index.
    ISBN 0-8092-4289-3
    1. Cookery (Oat bran)   2. Baking.   I. Glick, Ruth, 1942–
II. Title.
TX809.O22B34   1989
641.6'313—dc20   89-34902
                                                              CIP

Published by Contemporary Books, Inc.
180 North Michigan Avenue, Chicago, Illinois 60601
Manufactured in the United States of America
Library of Congress Catalog Card Number: 89-34902
International Standard Book Number: 0-8092-4289-3

Published simultaneously in Canada by Beaverbooks, Ltd.
195 Allstate Parkway, Valleywood Business Park
Markham, Ontario L3R 4T8 Canada

Contents

To Roc and Norman, our own favorite cholesterol counters!

Acknowledgments

We would like to thank The Quaker Oat Company for generously furnishing us with oat-bran cereal for use in this book. Also, there were a number of people who helped test recipes—most notably Joanne Settel, Elissa Glick, and Linda Hayes. Our tasters were also very important, as their helpful comments made it easier to refine our recipes. In particular, we'd like to thank the members of the Columbia Writers' Workshop and the personnel at the Office of the Chief Scientist, who carefully rated our efforts.

Introduction

Let them eat cake or a cookie—at least occasionally—and serve them food that tastes good: that was the challenge we took on when our husbands were told to reduce their serum cholesterol levels by making significant modifications in their diets. Specifically, both men were advised by their doctors to eat more oat bran and other foods high in fiber and to lower their consumption of fat.

Like everyone else, we were looking for an easy, painless way to make these changes. Yet despite the current media hype, we knew that cooking to lower cholesterol wasn't simply a matter of dumping some oat bran into a bowl for breakfast or consuming products with *oat bran* prominently advertised on the package. And oat bran–sprinkled doughnuts certainly weren't going to do the trick, either.

We knew that diet modification would require a comprehensive approach. As cookbook authors familiar with the nutrition literature and experienced at developing recipes that are both healthful and delicious, we were better equipped than most family cooks to take on such a task.

We began by surveying all the current nutritional strategies that seemed appropriate. Then, as a major part of our plan, we started designing oat-bran baked goods that were healthful but looked and tasted like "normal" food. Our goal was to produce dishes so appealing that family members would be able to stay with the new eating plan for life. In addition, we aimed for recipes whose preparation would fit easily into our own busy schedules.

With experimentation, we found we could make everything from great-tasting quick breads and muffins to wonderful cookies and cakes that were high in oat bran and other soluble fiber and low in fat.

But the proof is in the pudding. A cook's ultimate compliment is: "May I have your recipe?" Over and over, we have been asked to share the recipes in this book—even by people who aren't on special diets. Now we can share them with you, too.

1
Ingredients and Guidelines

We worked within a number of guidelines while developing the recipes in *The Oat Bran Baking Book.*

Limiting Fat

One of the major elements of any cholesterol-lowering plan is restricting fat—especially saturated fat. Thus we carefully designed our recipes to use as little fat as possible. Most call for only minimal amounts of low–saturated-fat vegetable oils such as safflower oil, corn oil, and olive oil. Also, alternating among these three provides a balance between polyunsaturated and monounsaturated oils.

A few recipes that require margarine call for the least-hydrogenated tub style. This is because hydrogenating oil turns it into saturated fat, which in turn tends to raise blood cholesterol.

Do not, however, use "diet" or "light" tub-style margarine to prepare these recipes as it has a higher water content and will not yield the expected results in baked goods.

Dairy Products

To avoid saturated fat even further, the only dairy products used routinely in *The Oat Bran Baking Book* are nonfat dry milk, skim milk, nonfat yogurt, and buttermilk made from skim milk. By the way, we've found that buttermilk is one of the most useful products there is for adding richness, flavor, and tenderness to baked goods.

Protein

Another reason we turned to nonfat dairy products is that they're an excellent source of protein—a real plus when the amount of meat (which is high in saturated fat) must be restricted in the diet. What's more, according to a number of studies, skim-milk products have the added benefit of actually helping to lower serum cholesterol.

Eggs

Eggs were one more ingredient we used judiciously. Egg yolks are fatty and high in cholesterol, but the whites are fat- and cholesterol-free and are a wonderful source of protein. Therefore, we call for whites only.

Nuts and Cheese

Oddly enough, many people seem to think that nuts and cheese are healthful ingredients—and they appear frequently in "healthy" recipes. However, both nuts and cheese are extremely high in fat. In fact, the fat in cheese is saturated. So we try to avoid these ingredients. Nuts are used as a garnish only on our Honey Almond Coffee Ring. And a little Parmesan in our Pizza Crackers and on our Mini Pizzas is the only cheese used.

Oat Bran

Of course, oat bran was a key ingredient in our recipes. An excellent source of soluble fiber that helps lower cholesterol, oat bran is convenient to use and easy to incorporate into baked goods because of its mild taste. We learned through experimentation, however, that oat bran can't simply be substituted for flour. Recipes overloaded with oat bran tend to be heavy, dry, and unpalatable. Even when a reasonable amount is used, further modifications in the ratio of ingredients are usually necessary for products to rise properly, taste good, and have a pleasant texture. (As with any fiber, remember to at first limit your intake while your system adjusts to the added bulk.)

Fine and Coarse Oat Bran

There are several different brands of oat bran on the market. Most are sold as *oat-bran cereal*. Some, like Quaker and Mothers, are finely ground and have a mild, pleasant flavor. We've found these particularly good for making cakes and other delicate baked goods. Others, like Sovex, Hodgson Mills, and brands sold in bulk, are usually coarser. These can be used in crackers and other baked goods where a bit of texture is desirable. If you happen to have a coarser variety and want to make a cake or other recipe calling for fine oat bran, first grind it in the food processor for several minutes.

A Few Special Techniques

Some of the techniques we used may seem a bit unusual. For example, because oat bran absorbs more liquid than flour, we sometimes combine it with wet ingredients and let the mixture stand for several minutes (while the other elements are being mixed together) to allow the oat bran to absorb moisture. This means that a higher percentage of oat bran than would otherwise be palatable can be used in muffins and quick breads. This mixing technique also helps keep the product from drying out later. In addition, with oat bran, the baking time often needs to be shorter than for conventional recipes.

Storing Oat-Bran Baked Goods

Because cakes, cookies, muffins, and other baked goods made with oat bran tend to dry out quickly, they should be stored in airtight containers or plastic bags. Since the recipes in this book are prepared with no preservatives, they often keep better if refrigerated.

Other Foods High in Soluble Fiber

As we developed recipes, we took full advantage of additional foods high in soluble fiber, including apples, carrots, and a variety of other fruits and vegetables.

Salt and Sugar

We also made our recipes low in salt and as low in sugar as possible—while still aiming for baked goods with the appearance, taste, and texture of "regular food."

Crackers

Incidentally, you may wonder why we have included a number of cracker recipes in the book. Commercial crackers are often high in fat and frequently contain saturated fats such as palm oil, coconut oil, or lard. But since crackers are a great snack food and a nice accompaniment to soups and stews, we've provided several easy recipes that are low in fat.

Recipe Testing

All of the recipes in this book have been carefully tested. The directions are clear and detailed so that you can be assured of good results in your own kitchen. In addition to baking times, we've given alternate indications of doneness because oven temperature and the temperature of the ingredients will vary. We also specify pan size as this greatly affects baking time.

What You Can Expect

Once we began gathering together material for this book, we set some further requirements. Our recipes:

- use only readily available ingredients
- are easy for home cooks to prepare
- appeal to typical American tastes
- incorporate time-saving shortcuts

Even given all our self-imposed restrictions, we came up with a whole array of products that really are "good for you and tasty, too." These range from Apricot Bread and Blueberry Muffins to Onion Crisps and Puffy White Rolls. In addition, we also devised a number of sweet treats for special occasions. These, like Chocolate Sheet Cake and Chocolate-Chip Oat Cookies, are designed to help keep people on a long-term, cholesterol-lowering regime from going off their diets or feeling deprived.

So browse through the selection of recipes we've devised. You'll probably find something you want to serve with dinner tonight or offer for breakfast tomorrow. You even have the option of baking a batch of delicious cookies or a guilt-free cake.

2
Quick Breads

◆ CRANBERRY BREAD ◆

Colorful, flavorful, and rich in healthful oat bran and fruit fiber.

> **3 cups fine oat bran**
> **1 6-ounce can orange-juice concentrate, thawed**
> **Finely grated rind of 1 large orange (orange part only)**
> **1¼ cups granulated sugar**
> **⅔ cup safflower, corn, or olive oil**
> **3 large egg whites**
> **1 tablespoon ground cinnamon**
> **½ teaspoon ground cloves**
> **2 teaspoons vanilla extract**
> **2 cups all-purpose or unbleached white flour**
> **1 tablespoon baking powder**
> **½ teaspoon baking soda**
> **½ cup skim milk**
> **2½ cups coarsely chopped fresh or frozen (thawed) cranberries (about 12 ounces)**

Preheat the oven to 350° F.

Combine the oat bran, orange-juice concentrate, orange rind, sugar, oil, egg whites, cinnamon, cloves, and vanilla extract in a large bowl, and stir until well mixed. Set the mixture aside for 5 minutes to allow the oat bran to absorb some of the liquid.

In a medium-sized bowl stir together the flour, baking powder, and baking soda until well blended. Using a large wooden spoon, stir the flour mixture into the oat-bran mixture until just combined but not overmixed. Stir in the milk and cranberries until distributed throughout. Immediately divide the mixture between two medium-sized (8″ × 4″ or similar), lightly greased or nonstick, spray-coated loaf pans, spreading batter out to pan edges.

Bake the loaves on the center rack for 30 to 35 minutes or until the tops are lightly browned and spring back when lightly tapped. Transfer the pans to a cooling rack and let stand for 15 minutes. Run a knife around the loaves to loosen them. Then remove them from the pans, and let them stand on the rack until thoroughly cooled.

Store the loaves in the refrigerator. (They may also be frozen for later use.) Slice using a large, sharp knife.

Makes 2 medium-sized loaves

◆ BANANA-ORANGE BREAD ◆

Considering how wholesome this bread is and how loaded with oat bran, it's remarkably light and appealing.

> 2 cups all-purpose or unbleached white flour (or 1 cup white flour and 1 cup whole-wheat flour)
> 3½ cups fine oat bran
> 1¼ cups granulated sugar
> ⅔ cup instant nonfat dry milk powder
> Finely grated rind of 1 very large orange (orange part only)
> 1¼ pounds very ripe bananas (3 large), cut into chunks
> ½ cup safflower, corn, or olive oil
> 3 large egg whites
> 1½ tablespoons baking powder
> ½ teaspoon baking soda

Preheat the oven to 350°F.

Stir together the flour, oat bran, sugar, milk powder, and orange rind in a large bowl until well blended. In a blender or food processor, combine the bananas, oil, and egg whites, and blend until liquefied and smooth. Pour all *except* ½ cup banana mixture over flour mixture and, using a large wooden spoon, stir until well mixed. Set the mixture aside for 10 minutes to allow the oat bran to absorb some of the liquid. Stir the baking powder and baking soda into the remaining ½ cup banana mixture. Stir the baking powder–banana mixture into the batter until well blended. Immediately divide the batter between two large (9″ × 5″ or similar), greased or nonstick, spray-coated loaf pans, spreading the batter out to the pan edges.

Bake the loaves on the center oven rack for 30 to 35 minutes or until tops are brown and spring back when lightly tapped. Transfer the pans to wire racks and let stand for 15 minutes. Remove loaves from the pans and return to racks until thoroughly cooled.

Store the bread in the refrigerator. Slice using a large, sharp knife.

Makes 2 large loaves

◆ PUMPKIN-SPICE BREAD ◆

The pumpkin adds flavor, moistness, and vitamin A to this hearty quick bread.

> 1 cup canned solid-pack pumpkin (not pumpkin-
>   pie filling)
> ½ cup skim milk
> ¼ cup safflower, corn, or olive oil
> 2 large egg whites
> 1 cup granulated sugar
> 2 cups fine or coarse oat bran
> 1 cup all-purpose or unbleached white flour
> 1½ teaspoons baking powder
> 1 teaspoon baking soda
> 1 tablespoon ground cinnamon
> 1¼ teaspoons ground allspice
> ¾ teaspoon ground cloves
> ¼ teaspoon ground nutmeg
> ⅛ teaspoon salt
> ⅔ cup dark seedless raisins or chopped dates

Preheat the oven to 375° F.

Stir together the pumpkin, milk, oil, egg whites, sugar, and oat bran in a large bowl. Let stand for 5 minutes. Thoroughly stir together the flour, baking powder, baking soda, cinnamon, allspice, cloves, nutmeg, and salt in a medium-sized bowl. Stir the flour mixture into the oat-bran mixture using a large wooden spoon. Stir in the raisins until incorporated throughout. Spoon the mixture into a thoroughly greased or nonstick, spray-coated, large (9″ × 5″ or similar) loaf pan, smoothing and spreading the batter out toward the pan edges.

Bake for 40 to 45 minutes or until the center of the top feels springy when tapped and a toothpick inserted in the thickest part comes out clean. Transfer the pan to a cooling rack and let stand for 15 minutes. Remove the loaf from the pan and return to the rack. Let stand until completely cooled.

Makes 1 large loaf

◆ DATE AND HONEY LOAF ◆

Dates and honey combine nicely in this loaf. Because the dates tend to sink in the batter, half of them are added to the top of the loaf before baking.

1 cup fine oat bran
1 cup water
1¼ cups all-purpose or unbleached white flour
⅓ cup instant nonfat dry milk powder
1½ teaspoons baking powder
½ teaspoon baking soda
1 large egg white
½ cup clover honey
¼ cup granulated sugar
2 tablespoons safflower, corn, or olive oil
½ teaspoon lemon extract
1 cup chopped pitted dates
2 teaspoons all-purpose or unbleached white flour

Preheat the oven to 350°F. Grease or coat an 8½″ × 4½″ loaf pan with nonstick spray. Line the bottom of the pan with wax paper. Set the pan aside.

In a small bowl, stir together the oat bran and water. Set aside to allow the oat bran to absorb the liquid.

In a medium-sized bowl, combine the flour, milk powder, baking powder, and baking soda. Set aside.

Put the egg white, honey, sugar, oil, and lemon extract in a large mixing bowl. Beat with an electric mixer on medium speed until well combined and smooth.

Add the oat-bran mixture and beat until combined. Gradually add the dry ingredients, continuing to beat until the batter is smooth.

Toss the dates with the 2 teaspoons of flour, coating the pieces well and separating any that have stuck together. Stir half the dates into the batter. Transfer the batter to the loaf pan. Sprinkle the remaining dates evenly on top. Bake for 51 to 57 minutes or until the loaf is golden brown and a toothpick inserted in the center comes out clean. Let the pan cool on a wire rack for about 10 minutes. If necessary, before removing the loaf from the pan, loosen by running a knife around the edges. Invert the pan on a wire rack to remove the loaf. Remove the wax paper. Turn the loaf right side up and allow to cool completely on the wire rack.

Makes 1 large loaf

◆ HARVEST FRUIT BREAD ◆

Plumped with figs, prunes, raisins, and dates and rich in oat bran, these dense, hearty quick-bread loaves are both tasty and healthful. Orange juice and spices bring out the flavor of the dried fruits.

2 cups (about 12 ounces) coarsely diced pitted
    prunes
2 cups orange juice
1 cup granulated sugar
$\frac{2}{3}$ cup safflower, corn, or olive oil
$3\frac{1}{4}$ cups fine or coarse oat bran
$\frac{1}{2}$ teaspoon lemon extract
3 large egg whites
1 tablespoon plus 1 teaspoon ground cinnamon
1 teaspoon ground allspice
1 teaspoon ground ginger
1 cup all-purpose or unbleached white flour
1 tablespoon baking powder
1 teaspoon baking soda
$1\frac{1}{4}$ cups dark seedless raisins
1 cup (about 6 ounces) diced figs
$\frac{1}{2}$ cup (about $3\frac{1}{2}$ ounces) diced dates

Preheat the oven to 375° F.

Combine the prunes and 1 cup of the orange juice in a medium-sized saucepan and bring to a boil over medium heat. Lower the heat so that the mixture simmers. Cook, uncovered and stirring occasionally, for 10 to 12 minutes or until the prunes are soft and all but about 1 tablespoon of the orange juice has been absorbed. Transfer the prune mixture to a food processor fitted with a steel blade. Add $\frac{1}{2}$ cup of the remaining orange juice, and process the prunes until they are pureed and smooth. Combine the puree, the remaining $\frac{1}{2}$ cup orange juice, sugar, oil, oat bran, lemon extract, egg whites, cinnamon, allspice, and ginger in a large bowl, and stir with a large wooden spoon until well mixed. Set aside for 5 minutes.

In a small bowl, thoroughly stir together the flour, baking powder, and baking soda. Using a large wooden spoon fold the raisins, figs, and dates into the oat-bran mixture. Then stir the flour mixture into the oat-bran mixture until thoroughly incorporated but not overmixed. Immediately divide the batter between two large (9″ × 5″ or similar), lightly greased or nonstick, spray-coated loaf pans, spreading the batter out to the pan edges.

Bake loaves on center rack for 30 to 35 minutes or until tops are dark golden brown and a toothpick inserted in the thickest part comes out clean. Transfer the pans to wire racks and let stand for 10 minutes. Remove the loaves from the pans and carefully return them to racks until thoroughly cooled. The loaves may be frozen for later use, if desired.

Makes 2 large loaves

◆ MARMALADE BREAD ◆

Orange marmalade, grated orange rind, and spices give this loaf a very good flavor.

1½ cups fine or coarse oat bran
¾ cup American orange marmalade or British
    Seville orange marmalade
½ cup orange juice
¼ cup safflower, corn, or olive oil
2 large egg whites
Grated rind of 1 large orange (orange part only)
¼ teaspoon ground cinnamon
¼ teaspoon ground cloves
¼ teaspoon lemon extract
1 cup all-purpose or unbleached white flour
⅓ cup instant nonfat dry milk powder
2 teaspoons baking powder
½ teaspoon baking soda
1 cup finely diced pitted prunes
1 tablespoon granulated sugar for garnish

Preheat the oven to 375° F.

Combine the oat bran, marmalade, orange juice, oil, egg whites, orange rind, cinnamon, cloves, and lemon extract in a large bowl, and stir until well mixed. Set mixture aside for 5 minutes to allow the oat bran to absorb some of the liquid.

In a small bowl stir together the flour, milk powder, baking powder, and baking soda until well blended. Using a large wooden spoon, stir the flour mixture and then the prunes into the oat-bran mixture until well combined. Immediately spoon the mixture into a large (9″ × 5″ or similar), lightly greased or nonstick, spray-coated loaf pan, spreading the batter out to the pan edges. Sprinkle the granulated sugar over the surface of the batter.

Bake the loaf on the center oven rack for 30 to 35 minutes or until the top is nicely browned and a toothpick inserted in the thickest part comes out clean. Transfer the pan to a cooling rack and let stand for 10 minutes. Carefully remove the loaf from the pan, and let it stand on the rack until thoroughly cooled. Store the bread in the refrigerator.

Makes 1 large loaf

Note: Seville marmalade lends a pleasantly bitter quality to the bread. It also yields a slightly less sweet bread.

◆ APRICOT BREAD ◆

Flecked with orange-colored bits of dried apricots, this easy bread is both attractive and delicious.

¾ cup diced dried apricots
1¾ cups fine oat bran
1⅓ cups commercial buttermilk
¾ cup packed light brown sugar
3 tablespoons safflower, corn, or olive oil
2 large egg whites
¼ teaspoon lemon extract
¼ teaspoon almond extract
1¼ cups all-purpose or unbleached white flour
1 teaspoon baking powder
¾ teaspoon baking soda

Preheat the oven to 350° F.

Combine the apricots, oat bran, buttermilk, brown sugar, oil, egg whites, lemon extract, and almond extract in a large bowl, and stir until well mixed. Set the mixture aside for 5 minutes to allow the oat bran to absorb some of the liquid.

In a small bowl stir together the flour, baking powder, and baking soda until well blended. Using a large wooden spoon, stir the flour mixture into the oat-bran mixture until well combined. Immediately spoon the mixture into a large (9″ × 5″ or similar), lightly greased or nonstick, spray-coated loaf pan, spreading batter out to pan edges.

Bake the loaf on the center oven rack for 38 to 43 minutes or until the top is nicely browned and a toothpick inserted in the thickest part comes out clean. Transfer the pan to a cooling rack and let stand for 10 minutes. Carefully remove the loaf from the pan, and let it stand on the rack until thoroughly cooled.

Store the bread in the refrigerator. Slice using a large, sharp knife.

Makes 1 large loaf

◆ BAKED BROWN BREAD ◆

The flavor of this hearty loaf is reminiscent of Boston brown bread. The texture is different, however, since this bread is baked rather than steamed.

2 cups fine oat bran
1⅔ cups commercial buttermilk
½ cup dark molasses
¼ cup clover honey
3½ tablespoons safflower, corn, or olive oil
2 large egg whites
1 cup dark seedless raisins
1 cup whole-wheat flour
1 cup all-purpose or unbleached white flour
1½ teaspoons baking powder
¾ teaspoon baking soda
¼ teaspoon salt

Preheat the oven to 350° F.

Combine the oat bran, buttermilk, molasses, honey, oil, egg whites, and raisins in a large bowl, and stir until well mixed. Set the mixture aside for 5 minutes to allow the oat bran to absorb some of the liquid.

In a small bowl stir together the whole-wheat flour, white flour, baking powder, baking soda, and salt until well blended. Using a large wooden spoon, stir the flour mixture into the oat-bran mixture until well combined. Immediately spoon the mixture into a very large (9″ × 5″ or similar), lightly greased or nonstick, spray-coated loaf pan, spreading the batter out to the pan edges.

Bake the loaf on the center oven rack for 40 to 50 minutes or until the top is nicely browned and a toothpick inserted in the thickest part comes out clean. Transfer the pan to a cooling rack and let stand for 10 minutes. Carefully remove the loaf from the pan, and let it stand on the rack until thoroughly cooled.

Store the bread in the refrigerator. Slice using a large, sharp knife.

Makes 1 large loaf

◆ APPLE-DATE BREAD ◆

In addition to fiber-rich apples and dates, apple juice and spices enhance this fragrant bread.

3½ cups fine or coarse oat bran
1¾ cups apple juice
1 cup packed light or dark brown sugar
½ cup safflower, corn, or olive oil
3 large egg whites
½ teaspoon lemon extract
1½ cups all-purpose or unbleached white flour
⅓ cup instant nonfat dry milk powder
1 tablespoon baking powder
1½ teaspoons baking soda
1½ tablespoons ground cinnamon
1½ teaspoons ground ginger
1½ teaspoons ground nutmeg
1½ teaspoons ground allspice
1½ cups peeled, finely diced Winesap, Rome, or
    other cooking apple
¾ cup finely diced dates

Preheat the oven to 350° F.

Combine the oat bran, apple juice, brown sugar, oil, egg whites, and lemon extract in a large bowl, and stir until well mixed. Set mixture aside for 5 minutes to allow the oat bran to absorb some of the liquid.

Stir together the flour, milk powder, baking powder, baking soda, cinnamon, ginger, nutmeg, and allspice until well blended. Using a large wooden spoon, stir the flour mixture into the oat-bran mixture until well combined. Fold in the apples and dates until evenly distributed throughout. Immediately spoon the batter into two large (9″ × 5″ or similar), lightly greased or nonstick, spray-coated loaf pans, spreading batter out to pan edges.

Bake the loaves on the center oven rack for 45 to 50 minutes or until the tops are nicely browned and a toothpick inserted in the thickest parts comes out clean.

Transfer the pans to a wire rack and let stand for 10 minutes. Carefully remove the loaves from the pans and let stand on the rack until thoroughly cooled.

Store the bread in the refrigerator (or wrap and freeze for later use). Slice using a large, sharp knife.

Makes 2 large loaves

◆ JEWISH HONEY LOAF ◆

Honey cake similar to this one is traditionally served at Rosh Hashanah, the Jewish New Year.

1 cup fine oat bran
½ cup strong brewed coffee
¾ cup warm water
1½ cups all-purpose or unbleached white flour
1½ teaspoons baking powder
1 teaspoon baking soda
¾ teaspoon ground cinnamon
Generous ¼ teaspoon ground allspice
Generous ¼ teaspoon ground ginger
⅛ teaspoon ground cloves
2 large egg whites
¼ cup granulated sugar
½ cup clover honey
2 tablespoons safflower, corn, or olive oil
½ teaspoon lemon extract
½ cup currants or dark seedless raisins

Preheat the oven to 325° F. Grease or coat a medium-sized (8½″ × 4½″ or similar) loaf pan with nonstick spray. Line the bottom of the pan with wax paper. Set the pan aside.

In a small bowl stir together the oat bran, coffee, and water. Set aside to allow the oat bran to absorb the liquid.

In a medium-sized bowl combine the flour, baking powder, baking soda, cinnamon, allspice, ginger, and cloves. Stir to mix well. Set aside.

In a large mixing bowl combine the egg whites, sugar, honey, oil, and lemon extract. Beat with an electric mixer on medium speed until well combined and smooth.

Add the oat-bran mixture and beat until well combined. Gradually add the dry ingredients, continuing to beat until just mixed. Stir in the currants.

Transfer mix to the loaf pan and bake for 63 to 68 minutes or until the loaf is golden brown and a toothpick inserted in the center comes out clean. Cool pan on a wire rack for 15 minutes. Invert the pan on the rack to remove the loaf. Remove the wax paper from the bottom. Turn the loaf right side up and allow to cool completely on wire rack.

Makes 1 large loaf

◆ IRISH SODA BREAD ◆

Since this traditional bread is made without fat and tends to dry out fairly rapidly, plan on eating it while it is still fresh.

1 cup fine or coarse oat bran
1¼ cups commercial buttermilk
3 tablespoons granulated sugar
1⅔ to 1¾ cups all-purpose or unbleached white
    flour
¾ teaspoon baking soda
½ teaspoon baking powder
Scant ½ teaspoon salt
¾ cup dried currants or dark seedless raisins

Preheat the oven to 375° F.

In a medium-sized bowl stir together the oat bran, buttermilk, and sugar with a large wooden spoon. Set aside for 5 minutes.

Thoroughly stir together 1⅔ cups flour, baking soda, baking powder, salt, and currants (or raisins) in a small bowl. Stir the flour mixture into the oat-bran mixture until blended. If the mixture is too moist, gradually stir in enough additional flour to yield a fairly firm, yet still slightly moist, dough. Knead the dough six or seven times, then form into a dome-shaped round almost 8 inches in diameter. Center the round in an 8-inch greased or nonstick, spray-coated round cake pan. Using a sharp, well-greased knife, cut 4-inch-long and approximately ½-inch-deep slashes horizontally and vertically across the loaf.

Immediately transfer the loaf to the preheated oven and bake for 30 to 35 minutes or until the top is firm and nicely browned. Remove the pan to a cooling rack and let stand for 5 minutes. Lift the bread from the pan and return it to the rack. Let stand at least 10 minutes longer. The bread may be served slightly warm or cooled. (It is good still warm but easier to cut when cool.) The slices may also be toasted.

Makes 1 medium-sized loaf

◆ CORN BREAD ◆

Corn bread is good served with chili or other spicy bean dishes.

> 1 cup yellow or white cornmeal
> 1 cup fine oat bran
> 3 tablespoons granulated sugar
> 2 teaspoons baking powder
> ¼ teaspoon salt
> 1 cup commercial buttermilk
> 3 tablespoons safflower or corn oil
> 1 large egg white

Preheat the oven to 425° F.

Combine the cornmeal, oat bran, sugar, baking powder, and salt in a medium-sized bowl. Stir to mix well.

Add the buttermilk, oil, and egg white to the dry ingredients and stir to mix. (Do not overmix.) Spread the batter evenly in the bottom of a greased or nonstick, spray-coated 9-inch square pan. Bake for 16 to 20 minutes or until the bread is firm and a toothpick inserted in the middle comes out clean. Corn bread tastes best served hot.

Makes 9 squares

Note: For a corn bread with fewer calories and less fat, reduce the sugar and oil to 2 tablespoons each. Be aware, however, that this version will dry out faster.

◆ FIESTA CORN BREAD ◆

Serve this spicy corn bread as a snack or with a Mexican meal.

1 cup yellow cornmeal
1 cup fine oat bran
⅓ cup instant nonfat dry milk powder
2 tablespoons granulated sugar
1 tablespoon baking powder
¼ teaspoon chili powder
¼ teaspoon salt
Pinch of cayenne pepper (optional)
3 tablespoons nondiet, tub-style safflower- or corn-
    oil margarine
1 cup water
1 large egg white
1 to 2 tablespoons canned chopped green chilies,
    drained
3 tablespoons chopped sweet red pepper (optional)
2 teaspoons instant (dried) minced onion

Preheat the oven to 425° F.

Combine the cornmeal, oat bran, milk powder, sugar, baking powder, chili powder, salt, and cayenne pepper (if used) in a medium-sized bowl. Cut in the margarine with a pastry cutter or two forks until well combined. Add the water and egg white, and stir in with a few swift strokes. Stir in the green chilies, sweet red pepper (if used), and minced onion.

Transfer the batter to a greased or nonstick, spray-coated 9-inch square baking pan, and spread out the batter to the edges of the pan. Bake for 17 to 21 minutes or until the corn bread is lightly browned and a toothpick inserted in the center comes out clean. Serve warm.

Makes 8 or 9 servings

◆ BUTTERMILK BISCUITS ◆

These are pleasantly light and flavorful. The dough is a bit soft to work with, but this yields tender biscuits.

¾ cup fine oat bran
1 cup commercial buttermilk
1⅔ cups all-purpose or unbleached white flour
2 teaspoons granulated sugar
2¼ teaspoons baking powder
¼ teaspoon baking soda
½ teaspoon salt
¼ cup nondiet, tub-style safflower- or corn-
     oil margarine

Preheat the oven to 425° F.

In a small bowl stir together the oat bran and buttermilk until well mixed. Set aside for 5 minutes to allow the oat bran to absorb the liquid.

In a medium-sized bowl stir together the flour, sugar, baking powder, baking soda, and salt. Cut the margarine into the dry ingredients using two forks or a pastry cutter until the mixture resembles fine meal. Stir the oat-bran mixture into the flour mixture until well combined, but do not overbeat. (The dough will be slightly soft.)

Lay the dough on a large sheet of wax paper. Cover with a second sheet of wax paper. Pat or press down the dough until it is about ½ inch thick all over. Gently peel off top sheet of wax paper, then replace paper loosely. (This allows dough to be easily lifted from paper later.) Turn the dough over and peel off and discard the top sheet of wax paper. Using a 2¼-inch or similar-sized cutter, cut out the biscuits; dip the cutter in flour after forming each biscuit, if needed, to prevent the dough from sticking to the cutter. Using a spatula, carefully lift the biscuits from the paper to a lightly greased or nonstick, spray-coated baking sheet, spacing them about 1 inch apart. (Dust the spatula with flour if the biscuits stick to it.) Combine the scraps and continue forming biscuits until all the dough is used.

Bake for 12 to 15 minutes, or until the biscuits are tinged with brown on top. They are best when served warm.

Makes 12 to 15 2½- to 2¾-inch biscuits

◆ BAKING-POWDER DROP BISCUITS ◆

With this recipe, you can have biscuits on the table in minutes. We like drop biscuits as a breakfast treat—or as an accompaniment to lunch or dinner. Serve them with preserves or marmalade.

1¼ cups all-purpose or unbleached white flour
1 cup fine oat bran
⅓ cup instant nonfat dry milk powder
1½ teaspoons baking powder
Scant ½ teaspoon salt
¼ cup nondiet, tub-style safflower- or corn-
    oil margarine
¾ cup water

Preheat the oven to 450° F.

Combine the flour, oat bran, milk powder, baking powder, and salt in a medium-sized bowl, and stir to mix well. Cut in the margarine with a pastry cutter or two forks until well combined. With a large spoon, stir in the water. The batter will be fairly wet.

Drop the dough by large spoonfuls onto a greased or nonstick, spray-coated baking sheet. Bake for 10 to 12 minutes or until the biscuits are lightly browned. Remove the biscuits immediately from the baking sheet.

Makes 11 or 12 biscuits

3
Muffins and Coffee Cakes

◆ BLUEBERRY MUFFINS ◆

The small amount of lemon extract in the batter brings out the flavor of these muffins. They're perfect for a Sunday breakfast or a company brunch.

1 cup all-purpose or unbleached white flour
1 cup fine oat bran
Generous ⅓ cup granulated sugar
1½ teaspoons baking powder
½ teaspoon baking soda
⅛ teaspoon salt
1 large egg white
1¼ cups plain nonfat yogurt
3 tablespoons safflower, corn, or olive oil
⅛ teaspoon lemon extract
Generous 1 cup fresh or dry-packed (unsweetened)
     frozen blueberries

Preheat the oven to 400° F.

Combine the flour, oat bran, sugar, baking powder, baking soda, and salt in a medium-sized bowl, and stir to mix well. Add the egg white, yogurt, oil, and lemon extract to the dry ingredients. Stir until just mixed. Gently stir in the blueberries. Divide the batter evenly among the 12 cups of a medium-sized greased or nonstick, spray-coated muffin tin.

Bake for 16 to 21 minutes or until nicely browned. Remove the muffins immediately to a wire rack. If the muffins are difficult to remove from the tin, rap the pan sharply against the edge of the counter to loosen.

Makes 12 muffins

◆ APPLESAUCE-OAT MUFFINS ◆

These are good! They are also high in fiber—from the oat bran, rolled oats, and applesauce.

1 cup fine or coarse oat bran
½ cup quick-cooking rolled oats
1 cup sweetened applesauce
½ cup plain nonfat yogurt
Generous ⅓ cup granulated sugar
1 large egg white
1 teaspoon ground cinnamon
¼ teaspoon ground allspice or cloves
1 teaspoon vanilla extract
3 tablespoons safflower, corn, or olive oil
⅔ cup all-purpose or unbleached white flour
1½ teaspoons baking powder
¾ teaspoon baking soda
⅛ teaspoon salt
½ cup dried currants or dark seedless raisins
2 teaspoons granulated sugar combined with ⅛
     teaspoon ground cinnamon for garnish

Preheat the oven to 425° F.

Thoroughly stir together the oat bran, oats, applesauce, yogurt, sugar, egg white, cinnamon, allspice, vanilla extract, and oil in a large bowl. Let stand for 5 minutes to allow bran to absorb some of the liquid.

Thoroughly stir together the flour, baking powder, baking soda, and salt. Using a large wooden spoon, stir the flour mixture and currants into the oat mixture until thoroughly blended but not overmixed. Divide the batter evenly within a standard-sized greased or nonstick, spray-coated muffin tin. (The tin will be almost completely filled.) Sprinkle the 2 teaspoons cinnamon-sugar over the muffin tops.

Bake the muffins for 13 to 16 minutes or until tinged with brown and springy to the touch.

Makes 12 large muffins

◆ APPLE-CARROT MUFFINS ◆

If you like, substitute a fresh peach for the apple in this recipe.

1 cup fine oat bran
1 cup all-purpose or unbleached white flour
⅓ cup granulated sugar
⅓ cup instant nonfat dry milk powder
2 teaspoons baking powder
½ teaspoon ground cinnamon
¼ teaspoon ground cloves
⅛ teaspoon salt (optional)
1 large egg white
Scant 1 cup water
2 tablespoons safflower, corn, or olive oil
1 medium-sized carrot, shredded or grated
1 large apple, cored, peeled or unpeeled, and
    grated or shredded

Preheat the oven to 400° F.

In a medium-sized bowl combine the oat bran, flour, sugar, milk powder, baking powder, cinnamon, cloves, and salt (if used), and stir to mix well. Add the egg white, water, and oil to the dry ingredients, and stir to incorporate, but do not overmix. Stir in the shredded carrot and apple. Divide the batter evenly among the 12 cups of a greased or nonstick, spray-coated muffin tin.

Bake for 18 to 23 minutes or until the muffin edges are lightly browned. Rap the sides of the pan sharply against the edge of the kitchen counter to loosen the muffins, or run a knife around the muffin edges. The muffins taste best warm but can be kept at room temperature for one or two days.

Makes 12 muffins

◆ EASY CORN MUFFINS ◆

These have a nice light texture and flavor.

> **1 cup yellow or white cornmeal**
> **½ cup fine oat bran**
> **1¼ cups skim milk**
> **1 large egg white**
> **3 tablespoons safflower, corn, or olive oil**
> **½ cup all-purpose or unbleached white flour**
> **¼ cup granulated sugar**
> **2½ teaspoons baking powder**
> **Scant ½ teaspoon salt**

Preheat the oven to 400° F.

In a medium-sized bowl stir together the cornmeal, oat bran, milk, egg white, and oil, and set aside for 5 minutes. Thoroughly stir together the flour, sugar, baking powder, and salt in a small bowl until well mixed. Gently but thoroughly stir the flour mixture into the cornmeal mixture. Divide the batter evenly among the 11 or 12 cups of a lightly greased or nonstick, spray-coated (or cupcake paper-lined) muffin tin.

Bake for 12 to 15 minutes or until the muffins are tinged with brown and springy on top. These muffins are best when served warm.

Makes 11 to 12 muffins

◆ BANANA MUFFINS ◆

A good way to use up ripe bananas.

> 1 cup fine or coarse oat bran
> 1 cup all-purpose or unbleached white flour
> 1½ teaspoons baking powder
> ½ teaspoon baking soda
> ⅛ teaspoon salt
> 1 large egg white
> 1 cup commercial buttermilk
> ¼ cup packed light brown sugar
> 1 large ripe banana, mashed
> 2 tablespoons safflower, corn, or olive oil
> 2 tablespoons clover honey
> ½ teaspoon vanilla extract

Preheat the oven to 400° F.

In a medium-sized bowl combine the oat bran, flour, baking powder, baking soda, and salt, and stir to mix well. Add the egg white, buttermilk, brown sugar, banana, oil, honey, and vanilla to the dry ingredients, and stir to incorporate, but do not overmix. Divide the batter evenly within a medium-sized, well-greased or nonstick, spray-coated muffin tin.

Bake for 16 to 19 minutes or until the tops of the muffins are lightly browned. Loosen the muffins by rapping the pan sharply against the edge of the counter. The muffins taste best warm but will keep for several days at room temperature.

Makes 12 muffins

Note: For a less-sweet muffin, 1 tablespoon of the honey can be omitted.

◆ PINEAPPLE-CARROT MUFFINS ◆

Good for breakfast, as a snack, or tucked into a lunch box.

1 cup fine or coarse oat bran
1 cup all-purpose or unbleached white flour
⅓ cup granulated sugar
2 teaspoons baking powder
½ teaspoon baking soda
1 teaspoon ground cinnamon
¼ teaspoon ground cloves
⅛ teaspoon salt (optional)
1 large egg white
1 cup commercial buttermilk
2 tablespoons safflower, corn, or olive oil
1 8-ounce can crushed pineapple, well drained
1 medium-sized carrot, grated or shredded
½ cup dark seedless raisins

Preheat the oven to 400° F.

In a medium-sized bowl combine the oat bran, flour, sugar, baking powder, baking soda, cinnamon, cloves, and salt (if used), and stir to mix well. Add the egg white, buttermilk, and oil to the dry ingredients, and stir to incorporate, but do not overmix. Stir in the pineapple, shredded carrot, and raisins. Divide the batter evenly within a medium-sized greased or nonstick, spray-coated muffin tin.

Bake for 17 to 20 minutes or until the tops of the muffins are lightly browned. Rap the sides of the pan sharply against the edge of the kitchen counter to loosen the muffins. The muffins taste best warm and fresh but will keep for one to two days.

Makes 12 muffins

◆ CRANBERRY MUFFINS ◆

Colorful and very tasty, these muffins make a nice addition to a holiday menu. They are also a perfect way to dress up an everyday meal. The cranberries have a pleasant tang and a flavor reminiscent of sour cherries.

1 cup plain nonfat yogurt
1 cup fine or coarse oat bran
Generous ½ cup granulated sugar
1 large egg white
3 tablespoons safflower or corn oil
1¼ teaspoons vanilla extract
⅛ teaspoon lemon extract
1 cup all-purpose or unbleached white flour
1¼ teaspoons baking powder
¾ teaspoon baking soda
½ teaspoon ground cinnamon
¾ cup coarsely chopped fresh or frozen (thawed)
    cranberries
1 teaspoon granulated sugar for garnish

Preheat the oven to 400° F.

In a large bowl stir together the yogurt, oat bran, sugar, egg white, oil, vanilla extract, and lemon extract and let stand for 5 minutes.

Thoroughly stir together the flour, baking powder, baking soda, and cinnamon in a small bowl. Stir the flour mixture into the yogurt mixture until incorporated but not overmixed. Gently fold in the cranberries. Divide the batter among the 12 cups of a standard-sized greased or nonstick, spray-coated muffin tin. (They will be full.) Sprinkle the 1 teaspoon sugar over the muffin tops.

Bake the muffins for 13 to 16 minutes or until tinged with brown and springy to the touch. The muffins are best served warm and fresh.

Makes 12 large muffins

◆ ORANGE-SPICE MUFFINS ◆

Fragrant and spicy.

> 1 cup all-purpose or unbleached white flour
> 1 cup fine oat bran
> 3 tablespoons granulated sugar
> 1½ teaspoons baking powder
> ½ teaspoon baking soda
> ½ teaspoon ground cinnamon
> ¼ teaspoon ground ginger
> ⅛ teaspoon ground cloves
> 3 tablespoons clover honey
> 3 tablespoons safflower, corn, or olive oil
> 1 large egg white
> ½ cup plain nonfat yogurt
> ½ cup orange juice
> ½ teaspoon grated orange rind (orange part only)
> ½ cup seedless golden raisins

Preheat the oven to 400° F.

In a medium-sized bowl combine the flour, oat bran, sugar, baking powder, baking soda, cinnamon, ginger, and cloves, and stir to mix well. Add the honey, oil, egg white, yogurt, juice, and rind to the dry ingredients, and stir to incorporate, but do not overmix. Stir in the raisins. Divide the batter evenly among the 12 cups of a medium-sized greased or nonstick, spray-coated muffin tin.

Bake for 16 to 18 minutes or until the tops of the muffins are browned. Rap the sides of the pan sharply against the edge of the kitchen counter to loosen the muffins. These muffins taste best warm.

Makes 12 muffins

◆ PUMPKIN-SPICE MUFFINS ◆

Don't sell pumpkin short—it's one of those healthful vegetables that deserves to be used more often. So try these spicy muffins. You can keep leftover pumpkin in the refrigerator for several days.

1 cup fine oat bran
1 cup all-purpose or unbleached white flour
⅓ cup granulated sugar
1 teaspoon baking powder
½ teaspoon baking soda
Scant ½ teaspoon ground ginger
¼ teaspoon ground cloves
¼ teaspoon ground cinnamon
⅛ teaspoon salt
1 large egg white
¾ cup plain nonfat yogurt
½ cup canned solid-pack pumpkin (not pumpkin-
    pie filling)
3 tablespoons safflower, corn, or olive oil
2 tablespoons clover honey
¾ cup dark seedless raisins

Preheat the oven to 400° F.

In a large bowl combine the oat bran, flour, sugar, baking powder, baking soda, ginger, cloves, cinnamon, and salt. Stir to mix well. Add the egg white, yogurt, pumpkin, oil, and honey. Stir just until mixed. Stir in the raisins. Spoon the batter into the 12 cups of a medium-sized nonstick, spray-coated or lightly greased muffin tin.

Bake for 16 to 19 minutes or until the muffins are springy to the touch and lightly browned.

Makes 12 muffins

◆ ZUCCHINI MUFFINS ◆

These have a pleasant, spicy flavor.

> 1 cup (unpeeled) grated or finely shredded
>   zucchini
> 1¼ cups all-purpose or unbleached white flour
> ¾ cup fine oat bran
> ¼ cup granulated sugar
> 1 teaspoon baking powder
> ½ teaspoon baking soda
> ½ teaspoon ground cinnamon
> ¼ teaspoon ground nutmeg
> ⅛ teaspoon ground allspice
> ¾ cup commercial buttermilk
> 3 tablespoons clover honey
> 1 large egg white
> 3 tablespoons safflower, corn, or olive oil

Set the shredded zucchini aside in a colander or sieve to drain. Preheat the oven to 400° F.

In a large bowl combine the flour, oat bran, sugar, baking powder, baking soda, cinnamon, nutmeg, and allspice. Stir until well mixed.

In a small bowl stir together the buttermilk, honey, egg white, and oil. Add the liquid ingredients to the dry mixture, gently stirring until the batter is thoroughly blended. Do not overmix. Stir in the zucchini. Divide the batter evenly within the greased or nonstick, spray-coated muffin tin.

Bake for 15 to 18 minutes or until the tops of the muffins are golden brown. Rap the sides of the pan sharply against the edge of the kitchen counter to loosen the muffins. These muffins taste best warm.

Makes 12 muffins

◆ HONEY-OAT MUFFINS ◆

If you're looking for nourishing, healthful oat-bran muffins with good flavor and texture but no refined sugar and very little fat, try these. The honey enhances the pleasant taste of the oats and lends the muffins just a hint of sweetness.

¾ cup quick-cooking rolled oats
1 cup fine or coarse oat bran
1⅓ cups commercial buttermilk
⅓ cup clover honey
1 large egg white
3 tablespoons safflower, corn, or olive oil
½ cup all-purpose or unbleached white flour
¾ teaspoon baking soda
¾ teaspoon baking powder
¼ teaspoon salt
⅓ cup dark seedless raisins or dried currants
    (optional)

Preheat the oven to 400° F.

Thoroughly stir together the oats, oat bran, buttermilk, honey, egg white, and oil in a large bowl. Let stand for 5 minutes to let bran absorb some liquid.

Thoroughly stir together the flour, baking soda, baking powder, and salt. Using a large wooden spoon, stir the flour mixture and raisins (if used) into the oat mixture until thoroughly blended but not overmixed. Divide the batter within the standard-sized greased or nonstick, spray-coated muffin tin. (The cups will be almost full.)

Bake the muffins for 14 to 16 minutes or until golden brown and springy to the touch. These muffins are best served warm and fresh.

Makes 12 large muffins

◆ QUICK RAISIN MUFFINS ◆

If you have our Homemade Pancake Mix on hand (see Index), these easy, fiber-rich muffins can be mixed up and in the oven in a matter of minutes.

1¼ cups Homemade Pancake Mix (see Index)
1 cup old-fashioned rolled oats
¼ cup packed light or dark brown sugar
¼ cup safflower or corn oil
1 large egg white
⅓ cup dark seedless raisins
1¼ cups commercial buttermilk

Preheat the oven to 400° F.

Thoroughly stir together the pancake mix, oats, and sugar until blended. Add the oil, egg white, and raisins, and stir until well mixed. Stir in the buttermilk until incorporated, but do not overmix. Divide the batter evenly among 11 or 12 lightly greased or nonstick, spray-coated cups of a muffin tin.

Bake for 13 to 16 minutes or until the muffins are slightly springy to the touch and lightly browned on top.

Makes 11 to 12 muffins

◆ STREUSEL COFFEE CAKE ◆

Another of our convenient from-homemade-mix recipes. Although this cinnamony treat is great with breakfast or brunch, it is also good served as a simple dessert. It keeps well.

STREUSEL
⅓ cup Homemade Pancake Mix (see Index)
⅓ cup packed light or dark brown sugar
¾ teaspoon ground cinnamon
3 tablespoons nondiet, tub-style safflower- or corn-
    oil margarine

DOUGH
1½ cups Homemade Pancake Mix (see Index)
¼ cup packed light or dark brown sugar
2 tablespoons safflower or corn oil
1 large egg white
¾ cup plain nonfat yogurt
⅓ cup dark seedless raisins (optional)

Preheat the oven to 350° F.

To prepare the streusel: In a small bowl, thoroughly stir together the pancake mix, brown sugar, and cinnamon until well mixed. Using a pastry cutter or two forks, cut in the margarine until it is evenly incorporated and the streusel is the consistency of coarse crumbs. (Alternatively, combine the pancake mix, brown sugar, and cinnamon in a food processor fitted with a steel blade. Process a few seconds to blend the ingredients. Sprinkle the margarine over the dry ingredients and process in on/off pulses until the margarine is incorporated and the streusel is the consistency of coarse crumbs.) Set the streusel aside until the dough mixture is prepared.

To prepare the dough: In a medium-sized bowl thoroughly stir together the pancake mix, brown sugar, oil, egg white, yogurt, and raisins (if used) until well mixed. Spoon the mixture into a greased or nonstick, spray-coated 9-inch *deep-dish* pie plate, or a 9-inch square or round baking pan with at least 2-inch-deep sides, spreading the dough out to the pan edges. Sprinkle the streusel evenly over the dough.

Bake for 25 to 30 minutes or until the streusel is melted and a toothpick inserted in the center of the coffee cake comes out clean.

Serve the coffee cake warm, directly from the baking pan. The cake can also be served at room temperature or reheated.

Makes 6 to 9 servings

◆ GOOD AND EASY CINNAMON COFFEE CAKE ◆

We like to serve this light and delicious coffee cake when friends gather in the afternoon or evening.

¼ cup safflower or corn oil
2 large egg whites
¾ cup granulated sugar
1 cup plain nonfat yogurt
1 teaspoon vanilla extract
1 cup all-purpose or unbleached white flour
1 cup fine oat bran
1 teaspoon baking powder
1 teaspoon baking soda

TOPPING
2 tablespoons granulated sugar
½ teaspoon ground cinnamon

Preheat the oven to 350° F.

In a large mixing bowl combine the oil, egg whites, and sugar. With an electric mixer on medium speed, beat in the yogurt and vanilla.

Combine the flour, oat bran, baking powder, and baking soda in a small bowl, and mix well. Gradually beat into the yogurt mixture until thoroughly combined but not overmixed.

Spread the batter in a well-greased or nonstick, spray-coated 8-inch ring pan (or a 9-cup Bundt pan or 9-inch square pan).

To prepare the topping, combine the sugar and cinnamon. Sprinkle the sugar-cinnamon mixture evenly over the batter.

Bake for 29 to 35 minutes or until a wooden toothpick inserted in the thickest part of the coffee cake comes out clean. Cool on a wire rack for 10 minutes. Loosen from the pan sides with a knife before removing. (If square pan is used, serve cake directly from it.)

Makes 8 to 11 servings

◆ MICROWAVE BLUEBERRY COFFEE CAKE ◆

This cake is easy to whip up, quick to bake, and quite tasty.

⅔ cup fine oat bran
⅔ cup sweetened applesauce
Generous ⅓ cup granulated sugar
¼ cup safflower or corn oil
2 large egg whites
⅔ cup all-purpose or unbleached white flour
¼ cup instant nonfat dry milk powder
½ teaspoon baking powder
⅛ teaspoon lemon extract
1 cup fresh or frozen (thawed) unsweetened
    blueberries

TOPPING:
1½ tablespoons granulated sugar
¾ teaspoon ground cinnamon

In a medium-sized bowl thoroughly stir together the oat bran, applesauce, sugar, oil, and egg whites until well blended; set aside.

Thoroughly stir together the flour, milk powder, and baking powder in a large bowl. Stir in the oat-bran mixture and lemon extract until thoroughly incorporated. Gently fold in the blueberries until distributed throughout.

Spoon the mixture into a lightly greased or nonstick, spray-coated 8-inch square microwave-safe baking dish, smoothing and spreading the top evenly out to the edges of the dish. Set the dish on a microwave-safe bowl or coffee cup in the center of the microwave oven. Microwave on high power for 2½ minutes. Turn the dish one-quarter turn and continue microwaving for 2½ minutes. Combine the sugar and cinnamon and sprinkle the topping mixture evenly over the coffee cake. Microwave for 4 to 5½ more minutes, rotating the dish one-quarter turn once during the baking period and continuing until a toothpick inserted in the center comes out clean. Set the baking dish on a heatproof surface until cooled.

Serve from the baking dish; cut into rectangles.

Makes 6 to 8 servings

◆ HONEY-ALMOND COFFEE RING ◆

Almond extract gives this coffee ring the flavor of marzipan. If pure extract is unavailable, artificial almond extract can be used.

CAKE
1 cup fine oat bran
1 cup commercial buttermilk
1½ cups all-purpose or unbleached white flour
1½ teaspoons baking powder
1 teaspoon baking soda
2 large egg whites
⅓ cup granulated sugar
⅓ cup clover honey
2 tablespoons safflower, corn, or olive oil
1½ teaspoons almond extract

HONEY GLAZE AND GARNISH
½ cup sifted confectioners' sugar
2 tablespoons clover honey
1 teaspoon skim milk
1 teaspoon nondiet, tub-style safflower- or corn-
    oil margarine
1½ to 2 tablespoons unblanched sliced almonds

Preheat the oven to 350°F.

In a small bowl stir together the oat bran and buttermilk. Set aside to allow the oat bran to absorb the liquid.

In a medium-sized bowl combine the flour, baking powder, and baking soda. Set aside.

Combine the egg whites, sugar, honey, oil, and almond extract in a large mixing bowl. Beat with an electric mixer on medium speed until well combined and smooth.

Add the oat-bran mixture and beat until well combined. Gradually add the dry ingredients, continuing to beat until smooth.

Pour the batter into a greased or nonstick, spray-coated 8-inch ring pan with a removable bottom.

Bake for 28 to 35 minutes or until the cake is golden brown and a toothpick inserted in the thickest part comes out clean. Do not overbake. Cool on a wire rack. When the pan is cool enough to handle, remove the cake from the pan and transfer to a plate.

Meanwhile, prepare the honey glaze. In a medium-sized bowl stir together confectioners' sugar, honey, milk, and margarine until smooth and well blended.

While the cake is still slightly warm, use a small spatula or table knife to spread the glaze over the top of the cake. Spread the glaze to the edges so that a small amount drips down the cake sides. Sprinkle almond slices over glaze.

Makes 8 to 12 servings

4
Yeast Breads

◆ OATMEAL BREAD ◆

These attractive loaves smell great as they bake and are nice for toast.

4 to 4½ cups all-purpose or unbleached white flour
2 packets fast-rising dry yeast
2 cups water
⅓ cup clover honey
¼ cup safflower or corn oil
1¾ teaspoons salt
1¼ cups fine or coarse oat bran
1¼ cups old-fashioned rolled oats
¼ cup instant nonfat dry milk powder

GARNISH
2 teaspoons old-fashioned rolled oats
1 teaspoon all-purpose or unbleached white flour

Stir together 3 cups of the flour and the yeast in a large mixing bowl. Combine the water, honey, oil, and salt in a small saucepan. Heat the mixture over medium-high heat to 125 to 130° F, stirring until the honey and salt dissolve. With the mixer on low speed, beat the liquid into the flour mixture until blended. Scrape down the sides of the bowl. Raise the speed to medium and beat for 5 to 6 minutes. Using a large wooden spoon, stir in the oat bran, oats, and milk powder until thoroughly incorporated. Scrape down the sides of the bowl carefully. Tightly cover the dough with plastic wrap and set aside in a warm place for 45 minutes.

Stir down the dough using a large wooden spoon. Vigorously stir in 1 cup more flour. Turn the dough out onto a lightly floured work surface. Dust the dough with a little flour. Knead for about 2 minutes, gradually working in enough additional flour to yield a malleable but not dry dough. Divide the dough in half.

With lightly greased hands, form each portion into a smooth, well-shaped loaf and transfer each to a medium-sized (8½″ × 4½″ or similar) greased or nonstick, spray-coated loaf pan. Lightly grease the tops of the loaves. Lightly sprinkle the top of each with the garnish mixture. Loosely cover the loaves with plastic wrap and set aside in a warm place for 35 to 45 minutes or until the dough rises slightly above tops of the pans. Meanwhile, preheat the oven to 375° F.

Remove and discard the plastic wrap. Bake the loaves in the preheated oven for 35 to 40 minutes or until the tops are very well browned and the loaf bottoms are firm and sound hollow when tapped. Let stand for 2 or 3 minutes. Remove the loaves from the pans and transfer to wire racks. Let stand until cooled. The loaves slice best when thoroughly cooled but taste great served still slightly warm from the oven. They will keep, wrapped airtight, for several days or may be frozen for up to 10 days.

Makes 2 medium-sized loaves

◆ ENGLISH-MUFFIN BREAD ◆

This no-knead breakfast bread has the taste and texture of English muffins but is much easier to make. The bread is also more convenient to toast than many English muffins, since it can be cut into slices that fit neatly into your toaster.

3½ cups all-purpose or unbleached white flour
2 packets fast-rising dry yeast
2⅓ cups water
3 tablespoons clover honey
2 tablespoons safflower or corn oil
Generous 1½ teaspoons salt
1½ cups fine or coarse oat bran
¼ cup instant nonfat dry milk powder
About ¼ cup yellow or white cornmeal for garnish

Stir together 3 cups of the flour and the yeast in a large mixing bowl. Combine the water, honey, oil, and salt in a small saucepan. Heat the mixture over medium-high heat to 125 to 130° F, stirring until the honey and salt dissolve. With the mixer on low speed, beat the liquid into the flour mixture until blended. Scrape down the sides of the bowl. Raise the speed to medium and beat for 5 to 6 minutes. Using a large wooden spoon, stir in the oat bran and milk powder until thoroughly incorporated. Scrape down the sides of the bowl carefully.

Tightly cover the dough with plastic wrap and set aside in a warm place for 40 to 45 minutes or until the mixture is very light and doubled in bulk. Meanwhile, grease or coat with nonstick spray two medium-sized (8½″ × 4½″ or similar) loaf pans. Sprinkle the pans with cornmeal and tip back and forth until the bottom and sides are coated. Set aside.

Stir down the dough using a large wooden spoon. Vigorously stir in the remaining ½ cup flour; the dough will still be fairly soft and rubbery. Divide the dough between the loaf pans, spreading it out to the pan edges. Sprinkle the tops of the loaves lightly with cornmeal. Loosely cover the loaves with plastic wrap and set aside in a warm place for 20 to 25 minutes or until the dough rises almost to the plastic wrap. Working gently so as not to deflate the dough, remove the plastic wrap, and let the loaves stand about 10 to 15 minutes longer or until the dough rises slightly above the tops of the pans. Meanwhile, preheat the oven to 400° F.

Gently transfer the loaves to the preheated oven. Bake for 25 to 30 minutes or until the tops are nicely browned and the loaf bottoms are firm and sound hollow when tapped. Transfer the loaves to wire racks. Let stand until thoroughly cooled. The loaves should be sliced and the slices then toasted before serving. The loaves will keep, wrapped airtight, for several days or may be frozen for up to 10 days.

Makes 2 medium-sized loaves

Note: For a wheat-raisin variation of English-Muffin Bread, substitute ½ cup whole-wheat flour for the ½ cup all-purpose white flour that is stirred into the dough after the first rising. Also, stir in ½ cup raisins along with the whole-wheat flour.

◆ NO-KNEAD MOLASSES-OAT CASSEROLE BREAD ◆

This is a hearty, full-flavored yeast bread. It is easy to make, since all the "kneading" is done with an electric mixer, and the dough requires no hand shaping. Like the other recipes in this chapter, this one also calls for fast-rising yeast, which makes the rising periods considerably shorter than for many yeast breads.

> 2 cups all-purpose or unbleached white flour
> 1 packet fast-rising dry yeast
> 1¼ cups water
> ¼ cup light molasses
> 1½ tablespoons safflower, corn, or olive oil
> ¾ teaspoon salt
> 1 cup fine or coarse oat bran
> ⅔ cup quick-cooking rolled oats
> ¼ cup instant nonfat dry milk powder
> ½ cup dried currants or dark seedless raisins
>   (optional)
> Additional ⅓ cup quick-cooking rolled oats for
>   dusting casserole and bread top

Stir together 1½ cups of the flour and the yeast in a large mixing bowl. Combine the water, molasses, oil, and salt in a small saucepan. Heat the mixture over medium-high heat to 125 to 130° F, stirring until the salt dissolves.

With the mixer on low speed, beat the liquid into the flour mixture until blended. Scrape down the sides of the bowl. Raise the speed to medium and beat for 4 minutes. Stir in the oat bran, oats, milk powder, currants, and remaining ½ cup of flour using a large wooden spoon; the mixture will be fairly stiff. Tightly cover the bowl with plastic wrap and set aside in a warm place for 40 minutes. Meanwhile, generously grease a 1½-quart round casserole. Dust the casserole with the ⅓ cup oats and tip back and forth to coat the interior evenly. Tap out the excess oats and reserve to sprinkle over the top of the bread.

Vigorously stir down the dough with a wooden spoon, and transfer it to the casserole. Spread the mixture out to the casserole edges, and smooth the top using a lightly greased table knife. Sprinkle the reserved oats over the bread top and pat down lightly.

Tightly re-cover the dough with plastic wrap and set aside to rise in a warm place for 30 minutes. Meanwhile, preheat the oven to 375° F. Remove and discard the plastic wrap. Let the dough stand in a warm spot for a few minutes longer, until it reaches the top of the casserole.

Bake in the preheated oven for 30 to 35 minutes or until the top is firm and the loaf sounds hollow when tapped. Remove the casserole from the oven and let stand on a cooling rack for 4 or 5 minutes. Run a knife around the bread to remove it from the casserole and return the bread to the rack. Let stand at least 15 minutes longer before serving. The bread may be served slightly warm, or cooled, cut into wedges. (It is good warm but easier to cut when cool.)

Makes 1 medium-sized loaf

◆ PUFFY WHITE ROLLS ◆

These rolls are large, light, and quite tender. Their wonderful texture results from the process of cutting the margarine into part of the flour, so do not alter this step.

3⅓ to 4 cups all-purpose or unbleached white flour
2 packets fast-rising dry yeast
1¾ cups water
¼ cup granulated sugar
1¾ teaspoons salt
¼ cup nondiet, tub-style safflower- or corn-
    oil margarine, cut into small chunks
1¼ cups fine oat bran
⅓ cup instant nonfat dry milk powder

Stir together 2 cups of the flour and the yeast in a large mixing bowl. Combine the water, sugar, and salt in a small saucepan. Heat the mixture over medium-high heat to 125 to 130° F, stirring until the sugar and salt dissolve. With the mixer on low speed, beat the liquid into the flour mixture until blended. Scrape down the sides of the bowl. Raise the speed to medium and beat for 2½ minutes. Place 1 cup of the remaining flour in a medium-sized bowl. Sprinkle the margarine over the top. Using a pastry cutter or two forks, cut the margarine into the flour until the mixture resembles very coarse crumbs; set aside.

Using a wooden spoon, vigorously stir the oat bran and milk powder into the yeast mixture until thoroughly incorporated. Stir the flour-margarine mixture into the dough until thoroughly incorporated. Scrape down the sides of the bowl carefully. Tightly cover the dough with plastic wrap and set aside in a warm place for 35 to 40 minutes.

Stir down the dough using a large wooden spoon. Vigorously stir in ¼ cup flour. Turn the dough out onto a lightly floured work surface. Dust the dough with a little flour. Knead for about 2 minutes, gradually working in enough additional flour to yield a malleable but not dry dough. Divide the dough in half. Then divide each half into 9 or 10 equal portions. With lightly greased hands, form half the portions into well-shaped balls and arrange, slightly separated and smoothest side up, on a greased or nonstick, spray-coated 9- or 10-inch pie plate or cake pan. Repeat the shaping and arranging process with the second half of the dough.

Lightly grease the tops of the rolls. Form a tent of aluminum foil over each pie plate, arranging it so that the rolls can rise about 1½ inches without sticking to the foil. Set the pie plates aside in a warm place for 30 to 40 minutes or until the rolls double in bulk. Meanwhile, preheat the oven to 375° F.

Remove and discard the foil. Bake the rolls for 13 to 17 minutes or until the tops are well browned. Transfer the pans to wire racks. The rolls may be served still warm from the oven, reheated, or at room temperature. They will keep, wrapped airtight, for several days or may be frozen for up to two weeks.

Makes 18 to 20 large rolls

◆ CINNAMON-RAISIN STICKY BUNS ◆

Everybody loves cinnamon sticky buns. Our version lets you indulge without overloading on fat and cholesterol and boosts oat-bran consumption at the same time.

DOUGH
3 to 3¾ cups all-purpose or unbleached white flour
2 packets fast-rising dry yeast
1¾ cups water
⅓ cup granulated sugar
3 tablespoons safflower- or corn-oil margarine
1 teaspoon salt
1⅓ cups fine oat bran
½ cup instant nonfat dry milk powder

FILLING
2 tablespoons nondiet, tub-style safflower- or corn-
    oil margarine
⅓ cup packed light or dark brown sugar
1 cup dark seedless raisins
1 tablespoon ground cinnamon

SAUCE
⅓ cup packed light or dark brown sugar
2 tablespoons dark corn syrup
¼ cup water
2 teaspoons nondiet, tub-style safflower- or corn-
    oil margarine

To prepare the dough: Stir together 2½ cups of the flour and the yeast in a large mixing bowl; set aside. Combine the water, sugar, margarine, and salt in a small saucepan. Heat the mixture over medium-high heat to 125 to 130° F, stirring until the sugar and salt dissolve. With the mixer on low speed, gradually add the liquid to the flour mixture, beating until just blended. Scrape down the sides of the bowl. Raise the speed to medium and beat for 5 to 6 minutes; the mixture will become rubbery. Using a large wooden spoon, stir in the oat bran and milk powder until thoroughly incorporated. Scrape down the sides of the bowl carefully. Tightly cover the dough with plastic wrap and set aside in a warm place for 45 minutes.

Vigorously stir down the dough using a large wooden spoon. Stir in ½ cup more flour. Turn the dough out onto a lightly floured work surface. Dust the dough with a little flour. Knead for about 2 minutes, gradually working in just enough additional flour to yield a malleable but still slightly soft dough. On a lightly floured work surface, roll out the dough into an 18- by 12-inch rectangle.

Spread the filling ingredients over the dough as follows: Coat the dough surface with the margarine using a table knife. Sprinkle the brown sugar, raisins, and cinnamon evenly over the margarine. Working from a longer side, roll up the dough jelly-roll style to form a long log. With lightly greased hands, gently stretch out the log until evenly thick and about 24 inches long. Using a large, sharp knife, cut the log crosswise into 24 1-inch slices. Arrange the slices just slightly separated in three lightly greased or nonstick, spray-coated 8-inch round cake pans or pie plates. Loosely cover each pan with plastic wrap and set aside in a very warm place for 35 to 45 minutes or until doubled in bulk. Meanwhile, preheat the oven to 375° F.

Remove and discard the plastic wrap. Bake the sticky buns in the preheated oven for 18 to 22 minutes or until the tops are lightly browned.

While the sticky buns bake, prepare the sauce as follows: Combine the brown sugar, corn syrup, and water in a medium-sized saucepan over high heat. Heat, stirring with a wooden spoon, until the sugar melts and the mixture comes to a full boil. Boil for 30 seconds. Remove the pan from the heat, and stir in the margarine until melted.

When the sticky buns are just lightly browned on top, remove the pans from the oven, and drizzle the sauce over them. Return the pans to the oven and continue baking for 3 or 4 minutes longer, until the sauce bubbles. Transfer the pans to cooling racks, and let the sticky buns cool slightly before serving. The buns will keep, wrapped airtight, for several days or may be frozen for up to 10 days.

Makes 24 3- to 3½-inch sticky buns

◆ SESAME BREADSTICKS ◆

These are great as a snack or served along with a salad and soup. We call for toasting sesame seeds in the recipe because this brings out their flavor.

3½ to 3¾ cups all-purpose or unbleached white
    flour
2 packets fast-rising dry yeast
1⅓ cups commercial buttermilk
¾ cup water
2½ tablespoons granulated sugar
1 tablespoon safflower, corn, or olive oil
1½ teaspoons salt
1¼ cups fine or coarse oat bran
½ cup sesame seeds (approximately)
1 large egg white beaten with 1 tablespoon water
½ teaspoon coarse salt (or table salt, if necessary)
    for garnish

Stir together 2 cups of the flour and the yeast in a large mixing bowl. Combine the buttermilk, water, sugar, oil, and salt in a small saucepan. Heat the mixture over medium-high heat to 125 to 130° F, stirring until the sugar and salt dissolve.

With the mixer on low speed, beat the liquid into the flour mixture until blended. Scrape down the sides of the bowl. Raise the speed to medium and beat for 5 to 6 minutes. Using a large wooden spoon, stir in the oat bran until thoroughly incorporated. Scrape down the sides of the bowl carefully. Tightly cover the dough with plastic wrap and set aside in a warm place for 40 minutes.

Meanwhile, spread 2 tablespoons of the sesame seeds in an ungreased skillet. Toast the seeds over high heat, stirring constantly, for about 2 minutes or until the skillet is very hot; then immediately lower the heat to medium. Continue toasting the seeds 1 to 2 minutes longer or until they are just barely tinged with brown and very fragrant. Immediately remove the skillet from the heat, continuing to stir the seeds. Transfer them to a small bowl. Lightly grease or coat with nonstick spray several very large (12″ × 16″ or larger) baking sheets. Spread about 1 tablespoon *untoasted* seeds on each baking sheet.

Preheat the oven to 450° F. Stir down the dough using a large wooden spoon. Vigorously stir in the *toasted* sesame seeds and ½ cup more flour. Turn the dough out onto a lightly floured work surface. Dust the dough with a little flour. Knead for about 2 minutes, gradually working in about 1 cup flour or enough to yield a smooth, fairly stiff dough.

Divide the dough in half. Working on a lightly floured surface and using a rolling pin, roll out each half into a 7½- by 12-inch rectangle. Lift the dough several times to make sure it isn't sticking. Working from a 7½-inch side, mark and then cut across the dough with a large sharp knife at ½-inch intervals to yield 15 12-inch-long strips.

Fold each strip in half, and then twist the two pieces together along the length. Pat or stretch the dough slightly to make the sticks evenly thick and about 10½ to 11 inches long. Transfer the sticks to a prepared baking sheet, spacing them about 1 inch apart. (If any sticks break, simply pinch them back together again.) Brush the tops and sides of the sticks lightly with the egg-white wash, one or two at a time, using a pastry brush or paper towel; immediately sprinkle the sticks with some of the reserved untoasted sesame seeds and coarse salt. Let the breadsticks stand for 5 minutes, then bake one sheet at a time.

Bake in the upper third of the preheated oven for 12 to 15 minutes or until the sticks are lightly browned on top. Lift the sticks from the pans using a spatula and transfer to the cooling racks. The sticks may be served warm or at room temperature. They may be kept a day or two or wrapped airtight and frozen for up to two weeks.

Makes 30 11- to 12-inch breadsticks

◆ MINI PIZZAS ◆

Quick, easy, and tasty, these mini pizzas are great for lunch with a salad or as a snack.

CRUST
2 to 2⅓ cups all-purpose or unbleached white flour
1 packet fast-rising dry yeast
1 teaspoon granulated sugar
½ to ¾ teaspoon salt
1 tablespoon olive oil
1¼ cups water at 125 to 130° F
1 cup fine oat bran

SAUCE AND TOPPING
1 cup canned tomato sauce
1 teaspoon garlic powder
1 teaspoon onion powder
1 teaspoon dried basil leaves
½ teaspoon dried oregano leaves
2 tablespoons grated Parmesan cheese

In a small bowl, combine 1¼ cups of the flour, the yeast, sugar, and salt. Stir to mix well.

Combine the oil and water in a large mixing bowl. Add the yeast mixture, and beat on medium speed for 2 minutes. Add ½ cup more of the flour and the oat bran. Beat on medium speed for 1 minute. Working in the bowl or on a clean, lightly floured surface, knead in enough additional flour to yield a malleable but still slightly sticky dough. Cover the bowl with plastic wrap and set aside in a warm place for 15 to 20 minutes.

Meanwhile, preheat the oven to 450° F. Make the sauce by combining the tomato sauce, garlic powder, onion powder, basil, and oregano in a small bowl. Stir to mix well. Set aside.

Knead the dough briefly. With floured hands, divide the dough into 12 portions. Working directly on a nonstick, spray-coated or greased baking sheet, stretch and shape one portion of dough into a flat, 4½- to 5-inch round. Repeat for each dough portion, forming 12 rounds. Divide the sauce evenly among the rounds. For each round, spread the sauce out evenly over the top surface, leaving a generous ¼-inch rim around the edge. Repeat for the remaining rounds. Sprinkle some Parmesan over each round.

Bake for 7 to 9 minutes or until the mini pizzas are slightly browned around the edges and browned on the bottom. Remove immediately to wire racks. Serve warm. Or cool the pizzas, wrap airtight, and refrigerate for several days or freeze for up to two weeks. To serve, rewarm mini pizzas.

Makes 12 mini pizzas

5
Cakes

◆ CHOCOLATE SHEET CAKE ◆

With this recipe, you really can have your cake and eat oat bran too. We like to serve this chocolate cake for company dessert because even guests who aren't on a cholesterol-lowering diet enjoy its chocolaty richness.

CAKE
1¼ cups all-purpose or unbleached white flour
¾ cup fine oat bran
1 teaspoon baking soda
¾ teaspoon baking powder
1 cup plus 2 tablespoons granulated sugar
½ cup plus 1 tablespoon unsweetened cocoa
    powder (not drink mix)
2 large egg whites
⅓ cup safflower or corn oil
1 cup commercial buttermilk
1½ teaspoons vanilla extract

DARK CHOCOLATE GLAZE
¼ cup plus 2 tablespoons granulated sugar
3 tablespoons unsweetened cocoa powder (not
    drink mix)
3 tablespoons skim milk
1½ teaspoons nondiet, tub-style safflower- or corn-
    oil margarine
½ teaspoon vanilla extract

Preheat the oven to 350° F.
In a large mixing bowl combine the flour, oat bran, baking soda, baking

58

powder, sugar, and cocoa powder. Stir to mix well. Add the egg whites, oil, buttermilk, and vanilla. Beat on medium speed until the ingredients are well combined and the batter is smooth.

Pour the batter into a greased or nonstick, spray-coated 11¼″ × 7½″ (or slightly larger) baking pan, spreading the mixture out toward the edges with a spoon.

Bake for 31 to 38 minutes or until the cake top is slightly springy to the touch and a wooden toothpick inserted in the center comes out clean. Transfer the pan to a rack and cool for 25 to 30 minutes.

To make the glaze, combine the sugar and cocoa powder in a small, heavy saucepan and stir until thoroughly blended. Gradually stir in the milk until well mixed.

Place the saucepan over medium heat and bring to a boil, stirring constantly. Boil, stirring, for 1½ minutes. Remove the pan from the heat. Add the margarine and stir until completely melted. Stir the vanilla into the glaze. Let the glaze stand for 3 to 4 minutes. Then quickly spread it over the warm, but not hot, cake with a knife or spatula. Let the cake stand until the glaze is cold. Cut the cake into squares and serve from the pan.

Makes 12 to 15 servings

◆ MOCHA CAKE ◆

If you love the combination of coffee and chocolate, here's the cake for you.

CAKE
1 cup fine oat bran
1 cup commercial buttermilk
1 cup all-purpose or unbleached white flour
1 teaspoon baking soda
¾ teaspoon baking powder
1¼ cups granulated sugar
⅓ cup unsweetened cocoa powder (not drink mix)
1 tablespoon instant coffee crystals
⅛ teaspoon ground cinnamon
¼ teaspoon salt
2 large egg whites
⅓ cup safflower, corn, or olive oil
1 teaspoon vanilla extract

MOCHA FROSTING
1½ cups sifted confectioners' sugar
¼ cup unsweetened cocoa powder (not drink mix)
2 teaspoons instant coffee crystals
1 tablespoon nondiet, tub-style safflower- or corn-
   oil margarine
3 tablespoons skim milk
1 teaspoon vanilla extract

Preheat the oven to 350° F.

In a small bowl combine the oat bran and buttermilk. Stir to mix well, and set aside to allow the oat bran to absorb the buttermilk.

In a large mixing bowl combine the flour, baking soda, baking powder, sugar, cocoa powder, coffee crystals, cinnamon, and salt. Stir to mix well. Add the egg whites, oil, vanilla extract, and oat bran–buttermilk mixture. Beat with an electric mixer on medium speed until the ingredients are well combined and the batter is smooth.

Pour the batter into a nonstick, spray-coated 9-inch square baking pan, spreading the mixture out to the pan edges.

Bake for 35 to 40 minutes or until the cake top is slightly springy to the touch and a wooden toothpick inserted in the center comes out clean. Transfer the pan to a rack and cool.

To make the frosting, combine the confectioners' sugar and cocoa powder in a small bowl. Set aside. Combine the coffee crystals, margarine, milk, and vanilla extract in a small, nonmetal cup. Microwave on high power for 35 to 45 seconds, until coffee and margarine are dissolved. (Or combine in a small saucepan and melt over medium heat, stirring, until coffee and margarine are dissolved.) With a spoon, stir the milk mixture into the confectioners' sugar mixture until well combined and smooth.

Spread the frosting on the cooled cake with a spatula or a table knife. Serve from the cake pan.

Makes 8 or 9 servings

◆ APPLESAUCE CAKE ◆

Applesauce adds moistness, great flavor, and fiber to this good, easy dessert cake. We make it often.

1 cup fine oat bran
3 tablespoons safflower, corn, or olive oil
1 large egg white
½ cup packed light or dark brown sugar
1 cup sweetened applesauce
⅓ cup dark seedless raisins
1 teaspoon vanilla extract
1 cup all-purpose or unbleached white flour
1 teaspoon baking powder
¾ teaspoon baking soda
1½ teaspoons ground cinnamon
½ teaspoon ground ginger
½ teaspoon ground allspice
⅛ teaspoon salt
2 tablespoons light or dark brown sugar for topping

Preheat the oven to 375° F.

Stir together the oat bran, oil, egg white, brown sugar, applesauce, raisins, and vanilla in a medium-sized bowl. Let stand for 5 minutes.

Stir together the flour, baking powder, baking soda, cinnamon, ginger, allspice, and salt in a medium-sized bowl. Stir the oat-bran mixture into the dry ingredients until thoroughly blended but not overmixed. Spoon the mixture into a lightly greased or nonstick, spray-coated 8-inch square baking pan, smoothing and spreading the batter out toward the pan edges. Sprinkle the remaining 2 tablespoons brown sugar over the batter top.

Bake for 22 to 26 minutes or until the center of the top springs back when touched and a toothpick inserted in the thickest part comes out clean. Transfer the pan to a rack and let stand until cool. Serve the cake from the pan, cut into rectangles.

Makes 6 to 8 servings

◆ ORANGE CAKE ◆

Moist and flavorful.

1¼ cups all-purpose or unbleached white flour
1 cup fine oat bran
1 teaspoon baking powder
1 teaspoon baking soda
¼ cup safflower, corn, or olive oil
2 large egg whites
Scant ¾ cup granulated sugar
1 cup orange juice
1 tablespoon grated orange rind (orange part only)
1 teaspoon vanilla extract
2 tablespoons packed light brown sugar for topping

Preheat the oven to 350° F.

Combine the flour, oat bran, baking powder, and baking soda in a small bowl, and mix well. Set aside.

In a large mixing bowl combine the oil, egg whites, and granulated sugar. With an electric mixer on medium speed, beat in the orange juice, orange rind, and vanilla.

Gradually beat the dry ingredients into the orange-juice mixture until well combined.

Spread the batter in a nonstick, spray-coated 9-inch square baking pan. Bake for 28 to 32 minutes or until the edges of the cake are browned and a toothpick inserted in the center comes out clean.

Sprinkle the brown sugar over the top of the warm cake. With the back of a large spoon or a table knife, spread the sugar out evenly. Cool cake on a wire rack. Serve from the pan.

Makes 8 or 9 servings

◆ CARROT-APRICOT BUNDT CAKE ◆

Not a traditional carrot cake, this large, impressive-looking version features both grated carrots and apricot-preserve glaze, as well as an optional powdered-sugar glaze.

BATTER
1¼ cups fine oat bran
½ cup safflower, corn, or olive oil
⅓ cup orange juice
3 large egg whites
⅔ cup packed light or dark brown sugar
1½ teaspoons vanilla extract
¾ cup apricot preserves
1½ cups all-purpose or unbleached white flour
1 teaspoon baking powder
¾ teaspoon baking soda
¾ teaspoon ground cinnamon
¼ teaspoon ground ginger
¼ teaspoon ground allspice
⅛ teaspoon salt
½ cup dark raisins
1½ cups finely grated or shredded carrots (about 2
    medium)
2 tablespoons light rum (or orange juice, if
    preferred)

ICING (Optional)
¼ cup confectioners' sugar
2 to 3 drops vanilla extract
¾ to 1½ teaspoons light rum (or water, if
    preferred)

Preheat oven to 350° F.

Stir together the oat bran, oil, orange juice, egg whites, brown sugar, and vanilla in a large bowl until well blended. Let stand for 5 minutes. Heat the apricot preserves in a small saucepan over medium heat until slightly syrupy. (Alternatively, heat the preserves in a glass measuring cup for 15 to 30 seconds on full power in a microwave oven.) Sieve enough of the mixture to yield ¼ cup of strained preserves; set the strained mixture aside for glazing the cake. Add the remaining preserves and the strained-out apricot pieces to the oat-bran mixture.

Stir together the flour, baking powder, baking soda, cinnamon, ginger, allspice, and salt in a medium-sized bowl. Stir the oat-bran mixture into the dry ingredients until thoroughly blended but not overmixed. Fold in the raisins and shredded carrots. Spoon the mixture into a very well-greased and floured 8-cup (or similar) Bundt pan, smoothing and spreading the batter out toward the pan edges.

Bake the cake in the preheated oven for 38 to 42 minutes or until the top springs back when touched and a toothpick inserted in the thickest part comes out clean. Place the pan on a wire rack and let stand for 15 minutes. Run a knife around the cake edges to loosen it from the pan. Transfer pan to the cooling rack, inverting it so that the cake "top" becomes the bottom. Let stand until cooled. Brush off any loose crumbs.

With the top still serving as the bottom, place the cake on a large round serving plate. Sprinkle the rum over the entire surface of the cake top. Using a pastry or basting brush or a paper towel, brush the cake top and sides with the reserved strained apricot preserves.

If icing is desired, in a small bowl stir together the confectioners' sugar, vanilla, and enough rum or water to yield a fluid, but not too thin, mixture. Drizzle the icing over the cake top, allowing it to drip down the sides. Let stand until the icing sets.

Makes 7 to 9 servings

◆ GINGERBREAD ◆

Moist, rich, and flavorful.

1⅓ cups enriched all-purpose or unbleached white
    flour
1 cup fine oat bran
1 teaspoon baking soda
1¼ teaspoons ground ginger
1 teaspoon ground cinnamon
¼ teaspoon ground cloves
¼ teaspoon salt
⅓ cup granulated sugar
⅓ cup nondiet, tub-style safflower- or corn-
    oil margarine
1 large egg white
1 cup light molasses
⅔ cup hot water

Preheat the oven to 325° F.

Combine the flour, oat bran, baking soda, ginger, cinnamon, cloves, and salt in a medium-sized bowl. Stir to mix well. Set aside.

Combine the sugar and margarine in a large mixing bowl. Beat with an electric mixer on low speed until lightened and smooth. Raise mixer speed to medium, and add egg white and molasses, continuing to beat mixture until incorporated. Add hot water, continuing to beat mixture until smooth. Gradually add the dry ingredients, and beat just until all of the flour mixture is incorporated into the batter.

Pour the batter into a nonstick, spray-coated 9-inch square pan. Bake for 40 to 45 minutes or until a wooden toothpick inserted in the center comes out clean. Serve the gingerbread from the pan, cut into squares.

If desired, serve with vanilla yogurt or frozen vanilla yogurt.

Makes 8 or 9 servings

◆ MICROWAVE GINGERBREAD ◆

This gingerbread keeps very well for several days at room temperature. In fact, it actually becomes moister on standing.

> 3 tablespoons nondiet, tub-style safflower- or corn-
>   oil margarine
> ⅓ cup packed light brown sugar
> ½ cup light molasses
> 2 large egg whites
> ½ cup commercial buttermilk
> ¾ cup all-purpose or unbleached white flour
> ¾ cup fine oat bran
> 1 teaspoon baking soda
> Scant 1 teaspoon ground ginger
> ½ teaspoon ground cinnamon
> ⅛ teaspoon ground cloves

Combine the margarine and brown sugar in a large mixing bowl. Beat with an electric mixer on medium speed until smooth and well combined. Beat in the molasses until the mixture is smooth. Beat in the egg whites and buttermilk. Combine the flour, oat bran, baking soda, ginger, cinnamon, and cloves in a small bowl. Beat into the margarine mixture until smooth and well combined.

Spread the batter evenly in a 9-inch round and at least 3-inch deep (or similar-sized) greased or nonstick, spray-coated glass casserole dish. Cover with wax paper and microwave for 5 to 6 minutes at 50 percent power, rotating the pan one-quarter turn halfway through the cooking period. Rotate one-quarter turn again and microwave on 100 percent power for 3½ to 4½ minutes or until the cake is puffed and a toothpick inserted in the center comes out clean. The center of the cake may still look slightly moist, but it will dry as it cools.

Makes 6 to 8 servings

◆ LEMON-GLAZED TEA LOAF ◆

A perfect addition to the tea or coffee table, this loaf cake is moist, flavorful, and very colorful. No one will ever guess that this is a high-fiber, low-fat quick bread.

LOAF
1 cup plain nonfat yogurt
1 cup fine oat bran
½ cup granulated sugar
2 large egg whites
¼ cup safflower or corn oil
1 tablespoon light or dark rum (or substitute
orange juice or water, if desired)
⅛ teaspoon lemon extract
Finely grated rind of 1 large lemon (yellow part
only)
⅔ cup dark or golden raisins
½ cup finely diced mixed, candied citrus peel, or
"fruitcake mix"
1 cup all-purpose or unbleached white flour
1¼ teaspoons baking powder
½ teaspoon baking soda
½ teaspoon ground cinnamon

GLAZE AND GARNISH
½ cup sifted confectioners' sugar
1 teaspoon lemon juice
2 teaspoons light or dark rum (or substitute
orange juice or water, if desired)
2 tablespoons diced candied citrus peel or candied
cherries and other decorative fruit pieces for
garnishing loaf top

Preheat the oven to 350° F.
Using a large wooden spoon, thoroughly stir together the yogurt, oat bran,

sugar, egg whites, oil, rum, and lemon extract. Stir in the lemon rind, raisins, and candied citrus peel, and let mixture stand for 5 minutes.

Thoroughly stir together the flour, baking powder, baking soda, and cinnamon in a small bowl. Stir the flour mixture into the yogurt mixture until incorporated but not overmixed.

Turn out the mixture into a greased or nonstick, spray-coated, large (9″ × 5″ or similar) loaf pan, spreading and smoothing the batter out to the edges.

Bake in the preheated oven for 37 to 42 minutes or until golden brown and springy to the touch. Transfer the pan to a cooling rack and let stand for 10 minutes. Run a table knife around the edge of the loaf to loosen, and remove it from the pan. Carefully return it to a rack set on a sheet of wax paper. Let stand until just barely warm to the touch before topping with lemon glaze.

To prepare the glaze, combine the confectioners' sugar, lemon juice, and rum in a small bowl. Mix until well blended and smooth. If the mixture is too stiff to spread, add a few drops of water until a spreadable consistency is obtained.

Using a table knife, spread the glaze over the cake top, allowing any excess to drip attractively down the loaf sides. Before the glaze sets, sprinkle the loaf top with 2 tablespoons diced candied citrus peel, or if desired, arrange candied cherries and other fruit pieces in an attractive pattern.

Makes 1 large loaf

◆ LEMON SNACK CAKES ◆

These snack cakes are good eaten plain, but for a special treat, they may be topped with the Honey-Lemon Glaze.

1¼ cups enriched all-purpose or unbleached white
    flour
¾ cup fine oat bran
1½ teaspoons baking powder
½ teaspoon baking soda
¼ cup safflower or corn oil
2 egg whites
¾ cup granulated sugar
1 cup plain nonfat yogurt
1¼ teaspoons lemon extract

HONEY-LEMON GLAZE
1 tablespoon plus 1½ teaspoons clover honey
¼ teaspoon lemon extract
1 teaspoon skim milk
1 teaspoon nondiet, tub-style safflower- or corn-
    oil margarine
¾ cup sifted confectioners' sugar

Preheat the oven to 375° F.

Combine the flour, oat bran, baking powder, and baking soda in a small bowl, and mix well. Set aside.

In a large mixing bowl combine the oil, egg whites, and sugar. With an electric mixer on medium speed, beat in the yogurt and lemon extract.

Gradually beat the dry ingredients into the yogurt mixture until well combined but not overmixed.

Divide the batter evenly within a muffin tin fitted with cupcake papers.

Bake for 17 to 20 minutes or until lightly browned. Remove snack cakes from muffin tin and cool completely on a wire rack.

To make Honey-Lemon Glaze, in a small nonmetal cup stir together the honey, lemon extract, milk, and margarine. Microwave on high power for 35 to 40 seconds or until the margarine is partially melted. Stir to mix well. (Or heat in a small saucepan over low heat, stirring, until the margarine is melted and mixture is smooth.) Stir the honey mixture into the confectioners' sugar until completely smooth and well blended. To ice cooled cupcakes, spread a thin layer of glaze on top of each, using a table knife or a small spatula.

Makes 12 snack cakes

◆ CHOCOLATE CUPCAKES ◆

Rich and chocolaty, these cupcakes are delicious eaten without icing. However, if desired, top them with the Chocolate Icing.

> 1 cup all-purpose or unbleached white flour
> 1 cup fine oat bran
> 1 teaspoon baking powder
> ¾ teaspoon baking soda
> 1 cup plus 2 tablespoons granulated sugar
> ½ cup unsweetened cocoa powder (not drink mix)
> ⅛ teaspoon salt
> 2 large egg whites
> ⅓ cup safflower or corn oil
> 1 cup commercial buttermilk
> 2 teaspoons vanilla extract

CHOCOLATE ICING
1 cup sifted confectioners' sugar
3 tablespoons unsweetened cocoa powder (not drink mix)
1 tablespoon nondiet, tub-style safflower- or corn-oil margarine
2 tablespoons skim milk
½ teaspoon vanilla extract

Preheat the oven to 375° F.

In a large mixing bowl combine the flour, oat bran, baking powder, baking soda, sugar, cocoa powder, and salt. Stir to mix well. Add the egg whites, oil, buttermilk, and vanilla extract. Beat on medium speed with an electric mixer just until the batter is smooth.

Divide the batter evenly among 12 *large* cups of a muffin tin fitted with large cupcake papers. (Alternatively, batter may be divided among 13 or 14 medium-sized cups of a muffin tin fitted with medium-sized cupcake papers.)

Bake for 19 to 24 minutes or until the cupcakes are slightly springy to the touch and a wooden toothpick inserted in the center of a cupcake comes out clean. (Bake medium-sized cupcakes 18 to 22 minutes.)

As soon as the cupcakes are cool enough to handle, remove them from the muffin tin and cool on a wire rack. Meanwhile, if desired, prepare the icing. Ice the cupcakes when cooled.

To make the icing, combine the confectioners' sugar and cocoa powder in a small bowl and mix well.

In a small nonmetal cup, combine the margarine, milk, and vanilla extract. Microwave on high power for 40 to 50 seconds or until the margarine is partially melted. Stir to mix well. (Or heat in a small saucepan over low heat, stirring, until the margarine is melted and the mixture is smooth.) Stir the margarine mixture into the confectioners' sugar mixture until completely smooth and well blended.

Spread the icing on the cupcakes with a small spatula or table knife.

Makes 12 large cupcakes

6
Cookies, Bars, and Brownies

◆ OATMEAL-RAISIN DROP COOKIES ◆

1 cup fine or coarse oat bran
½ cup all-purpose or unbleached white flour
¾ teaspoon baking powder
½ teaspoon baking soda
½ teaspoon ground cinnamon
¼ teaspoon ground nutmeg
¼ cup safflower or corn oil
⅔ cup packed light brown sugar
1 large egg white
¼ cup skim milk
1½ teaspoons vanilla extract
1 cup dark seedless raisins, chopped
1 cup old-fashioned or quick-cooking rolled oats

Preheat the oven to 375° F.

Thoroughly stir together the oat bran, flour, baking powder, baking soda, cinnamon, and nutmeg; set aside. In a large mixing bowl combine the oil, brown sugar, and egg white, and beat on medium speed until lightened and smooth. Beat in the milk and vanilla until thoroughly incorporated. Beat in the flour mixture until incorporated but not overmixed. Stir in the raisins and rolled oats using a large wooden spoon.

Drop the dough by generous rounded teaspoonfuls about 2½ inches apart on lightly greased or nonstick, spray-coated baking sheets. Using the blade of a lightly greased table knife, smooth and flatten the tops of the cookies just slightly.

Bake the cookies in the upper third of the oven for 8 to 10 minutes or until just slightly tinged with brown on top and at the edges. Remove pans from the oven and let stand for 1 minute. Using a spatula, transfer cookies to rack for cooling. Store airtight for two or three days. Freeze for longer storage.

Makes about 30 2¼-inch cookies

◆ CHOCOLATE-CHIP OAT COOKIES ◆

Chocolate-chip cookies aren't usually on the menu for people on a reduced-fat or cholesterol-lowering diet, and even a high-fiber version such as this should be considered a special treat. However, if you're simply interested in increasing the oat bran in your diet or in eating the most healthful but still delicious chocolate-chip cookie around, this recipe is it! (As an extra fat-reducing measure, carob chips can be substituted for chocolate chips, although the taste will not be quite the same.)

¾ cup quick-cooking or old-fashioned rolled oats
1 cup fine or coarse oat bran
1 cup all-purpose or unbleached white flour
1 teaspoon baking soda
¾ teaspoon baking powder
½ cup nondiet, tub-style safflower- or corn-
   oil margarine
⅔ cup packed dark brown sugar
⅓ cup granulated sugar
1 large egg white
2 teaspoons vanilla extract
1 cup (6 ounces) semisweet chocolate bits

Preheat the oven to 375° F.

Grind the rolled oats to a powder using a food processor or blender. (If a blender is used, stop motor several times and stir to redistribute oats.) Thoroughly stir together the ground oats, oat bran, flour, baking soda, and baking powder in a bowl until well mixed.

Beat the margarine, brown sugar, and granulated sugar in a mixing bowl with mixer on medium speed until light and smooth. Add the egg white and vanilla, and continue beating until well blended. Beating on low speed, add about half the dry ingredients until mixed. Stir in the remaining dry ingredients and chocolate bits by hand, until thoroughly incorporated but not overmixed.

Form cookies by pulling off portions of dough and shaping into scant 1-inch balls. Lay the balls about 2 inches apart on greased or nonstick, spray-coated baking sheets. Dip the bottom of a flat-bottomed drinking glass into cold water and shake off any excess water. Then press down each ball with the glass until it is about ¼ inch thick and 1¾ inches in diameter. Continue dipping the bottom of the glass into the water after forming each cookie to prevent the dough from sticking to the glass.

Bake the cookies for 8 to 9 minutes or until they are just barely tinged with brown at the edges. (They may seem very soft and slightly underdone but will firm up as they cool.) Remove the sheets from the oven and let stand for 2 minutes. Using a spatula, transfer the cookies to cooling racks; let stand until cooled. Store the cookies airtight. They can be kept for up to a week.

Makes 35 to 40 2½- to 2¾-inch cookies

◆ PEANUT BUTTER–CHOCOLATE CHEWS ◆

Attractive, slightly chewy cookies with an appealing peanut butter and chocolate flavor.

1 cup all-purpose or unbleached white flour
¾ cup fine or coarse oat bran
1¼ teaspoons baking powder
½ teaspoon baking soda
⅛ teaspoon salt
¼ cup safflower or corn oil
3 tablespoons smooth or chunky-style peanut butter
¾ cup confectioners' sugar
½ cup packed light or dark brown sugar
1 large egg white
2 tablespoons skim milk
1½ teaspoons vanilla extract
¼ cup unsweetened cocoa powder (not drink mix)

Preheat the oven to 375° F.

Thoroughly stir together the flour, oat bran, baking powder, baking soda, and salt; set aside. In a large mixing bowl combine the oil, peanut butter, confectioners' sugar, brown sugar, and egg white, and beat until lightened and well blended. Beat in the milk, vanilla, and cocoa powder until thoroughly incorporated and smooth. Beat in half the dry ingredients until thoroughly mixed. Stir in the rest of the dry ingredients using a large wooden spoon.

Cover and refrigerate the dough for at least 30 minutes (and up to 1 hour) or until firm enough to shape with the hands into balls. Shape the dough into 1¼-inch balls. Space them about 2 inches apart on greased baking sheets. Using the tines of a fork dipped in cold water, press down vertically and then horizontally on each cookie to form a marked round about 1¾ inches in diameter.

Bake the cookies in the upper third of the oven for 8 to 10 minutes or until almost firm on top and just beginning to brown at the edges. Remove the pans from the oven and let stand for 1 minute. Using a spatula, transfer cookies to cooling racks and let stand until thoroughly cooled. Store airtight for up to a week. Freeze for longer storage.

Makes about 35 2½-inch cookies

◆ MOLASSES COOKIES ◆

Be sure not to overbake these cookies if you want the texture to be slightly chewy. They're among our favorites and keep very well for several days.

½ cup nondict, tub-style safflower- or corn-
    oil margarine
⅔ cup granulated sugar
¼ cup light molasses
1 large egg white
¼ teaspoon lemon extract
1 cup all-purpose or unbleached white flour
1 cup fine oat bran
1 teaspoon baking powder
½ teaspoon baking soda
1 teaspoon ground cinnamon
½ teaspoon ground ginger
¼ teaspoon ground cloves
⅛ teaspoon salt

Combine the margarine and sugar in a large mixing bowl. Beat with an electric mixer on medium speed until light and smooth. Add the molasses, egg white, and lemon extract. Beat until well mixed.

In a small bowl combine the flour, oat bran, baking powder, baking soda, cinnamon, ginger, cloves, and salt. Stir to mix well. Add to the molasses mixture and beat until well combined. Cover the dough and refrigerate for 45 to 50 minutes, until dough is chilled and slightly stiff.

Preheat the oven to 375° F.

With your fingers, form the dough into 1-inch balls and place on a well-greased or nonstick, spray-coated baking sheet about 2 inches apart. (For subsequent batches, allow the baking sheets to cool thoroughly before reusing. Also, keep the dough refrigerated until needed.) Bake for 9 to 11 minutes or until spread and very lightly browned. Do not overbake. The cookies should be soft when taken out of the oven. Allow the cookies to cool on the baking sheet 1 or 2 minutes, then use a spatula to carefully remove them to a wire rack. Cool completely. When cooled, store in an airtight container.

Makes about 35 medium-sized cookies

◆ OLD-FASHIONED OATMEAL COOKIES ◆

These are mild, crispy, and high in fiber, from both the oat bran and the rolled oats.

¾ cup all-purpose or unbleached white flour
½ teaspoon baking soda
½ teaspoon ground cinnamon
⅓ cup nondiet, tub-style safflower- or corn-
  oil margarine
⅔ cup packed dark brown sugar
1 large egg white
2 tablespoons skim milk
2 teaspoons vanilla extract
1¼ cups fine or coarse oat bran
1 cup old-fashioned rolled oats
2 tablespoons sugar mixed with ¼ teaspoon ground
  cinnamon for garnishing cookies

Preheat the oven to 375° F.

Thoroughly stir together the flour, baking soda, and cinnamon; set aside. In a large mixing bowl combine the margarine, brown sugar, egg white, skim milk, and vanilla, and beat until lightened and smooth. Beat in the oat bran and let stand 2 to 3 minutes. Beat in the flour mixture until incorporated but not overmixed. Stir in the rolled oats using a large wooden spoon.

Cover and refrigerate the dough for about 15 minutes or until it is cool and firm enough to be formed into balls. Then shape the dough into 1¼-inch balls, and space them about 2½ inches apart on baking sheets. Dip the bottom of a large glass in cold water and shake off any excess water. Then press down on each ball to form a 1½-inch round. Repeat the process of dipping the glass in water and shaking off the excess before pressing each cookie, to prevent sticking. Sprinkle the cookie tops lightly with the sugar-cinnamon mixture.

Bake the cookies in the upper third of the oven for 8 to 10 minutes or until just slightly darkened at the edges. Remove the pans from the oven and let stand for 1 minute. Using a spatula, transfer cookies to cooling racks and let stand until cooled. Store airtight for up to a week. Freeze for longer storage.

Makes about 35 to 40 2½-inch cookies

◆ DATE DROP COOKIES ◆

Dates make these tasty cookies chewy and moist, and spices give them rich flavor and aroma. Choose plump, moist dates for best results.

These cookies keep well.

1¼ cups fine oat bran
¾ cup all-purpose or unbleached white flour
½ teaspoon baking soda
½ teaspoon baking powder
1¼ teaspoons ground cinnamon
1 teaspoon ground cloves
⅓ cup nondiet, tub-style safflower- or corn-
    oil margarine
⅔ cup granulated sugar
1 large egg white
3 tablespoons orange juice
1½ teaspoons vanilla extract
2 cups (about 10 ounces) pitted, diced dates

Preheat the oven to 375° F.

Thoroughly stir together the oat bran, flour, baking soda, baking powder, cinnamon, and cloves; set aside. In a large mixing bowl beat the margarine, sugar, and egg white on medium speed until lightened and smooth. Beat in the orange juice and vanilla until incorporated. Beat in about half the flour mixture. Using a large wooden spoon, stir in the rest of the flour mixture and the dates until distributed throughout.

Drop the mixture by generous teaspoonfuls onto lightly greased or nonstick, spray-coated baking sheets, spacing the cookies about 2½ inches apart.

Bake the cookies in the upper third of the oven for 8 to 10 minutes or until lightly tinged with brown. Remove the pans from the oven and let stand for 3 minutes. Then carefully transfer the cookies to cooling racks and let stand until cooled. Since the cookies may tend to stick together upon storage, it's best to pack them flat, with wax paper between the layers. Store the cookies airtight for up to four or five days. They may be frozen for longer storage.

Makes about 35 to 40 2¼-inch cookies

◆ COCOA ICEBOX COOKIES ◆

Like most icebox cookies, these are extremely convenient. The dough is made ahead, shaped into logs, and stashed in the freezer. Then, the still-frozen logs can quickly be cut into cookie slices and baked as needed.

$1\frac{1}{4}$ cups fine oat bran
$\frac{3}{4}$ cup all-purpose or unbleached white flour
$1\frac{1}{2}$ teaspoons baking powder
$\frac{1}{2}$ teaspoon baking soda
$\frac{1}{8}$ teaspoon salt
$\frac{1}{3}$ cup corn oil or safflower oil
$\frac{2}{3}$ cup confectioners' sugar
$\frac{1}{2}$ cup packed light or dark brown sugar
1 large egg white
$2\frac{1}{2}$ tablespoons skim milk
$1\frac{1}{2}$ teaspoons vanilla extract
$\frac{1}{3}$ cup unsweetened cocoa powder (not drink mix)

Thoroughly stir together the oat bran, flour, baking powder, baking soda, and salt; set aside. In a large mixing bowl combine the oil, confectioners' sugar, brown sugar, and egg white, and beat on medium speed until lightened and smooth. Beat in the milk, vanilla, and cocoa powder until thoroughly incorporated and smooth. Beat in half the dry ingredients until thoroughly mixed. Stir in the rest of the dry ingredients using a large wooden spoon. Cover and refrigerate dough 15 to 20 minutes or until firm enough to handle.

Divide the dough in half and place each portion on a sheet of wax paper. Shape each half into a log about 2 inches in diameter and 7 inches long. (It is easiest to smooth and finish shaping the logs by wrapping them in the wax paper and rolling them back and forth on the work surface.) Carefully transfer the logs to a tray or baking sheet, and place them in the freezer until completely frozen—at least 2 hours. The logs can be wrapped airtight and frozen for up to a week prior to baking.

To bake, preheat the oven to 350° F. Cut the still-frozen logs crosswise into scant $\frac{1}{4}$-inch slices using a large, sharp knife. Space them about $1\frac{1}{2}$ inches apart on lightly greased or nonstick, spray-coated baking sheets.

Bake the cookies for 6 to 9 minutes or until they are almost firm when touched in the center with a finger; be careful not to overbake. (Baking time will vary quite a bit depending on the coldness of the slices when placed in the oven.) Remove the baking sheets from the oven and let stand for 2 minutes or until the cookies have firmed up slightly. Using a spatula, carefully transfer the cookies to wire racks and let stand until cooled.

Store airtight for three or four days. Freeze for longer storage.

Makes 45 to 50 2¾-inch cookies

◆ GINGERSNAPS ◆

Zippy and robust in flavor, these are crunchy-crisp.

1¼ cups all-purpose or unbleached white flour
1 cup fine oat bran
2½ teaspoons ground ginger
1½ teaspoons ground cinnamon
½ teaspoon ground cloves
¼ teaspoon ground allspice
1¼ teaspoons baking powder
½ teaspoon baking soda
⅓ cup nondiet, tub-style safflower- or corn-
    oil margarine
⅓ cup light or dark molasses
½ cup granulated sugar
1 large egg white
1 teaspoon vanilla extract
Approximately 2 tablespoons granulated sugar for
    forming cookies

Preheat the oven to 375°F.

Thoroughly stir together the flour, oat bran, ginger, cinnamon, cloves, allspice, baking powder, and baking soda; set aside. Beat together the margarine, molasses, ½ cup sugar, egg white, and vanilla in a large mixing bowl on medium speed until well blended and smooth. Beat in half the dry ingredients. Stir in the remaining dry ingredients using a large wooden spoon.

To form cookies, pull off portions of dough and shape into scant 1-inch balls. Lay the balls about 1½ inches apart on greased or nonstick, spray-coated baking sheets. Lightly grease the bottom of a flat-bottomed drinking glass and dip the surface into the 2 tablespoons sugar. Flatten the balls with the glass until about ¼ inch thick and 1¾ inches in diameter. Continue dipping the bottom of the glass into the sugar after each cookie to prevent the dough from sticking to the surface.

Bake the cookies for 6 to 8 minutes or until they are just barely tinged around the edges and are almost firm on top. (The longer the baking time, the crunchier the cookies will be.) Remove the sheets from the oven and let stand for 1½ minutes. Using a spatula, transfer the cookies to racks and let stand until completely cooled. Store the cookies airtight. They may be kept for up to two weeks.

Makes 45 to 50 2¼-inch cookies

◆ FILLED FIG COOKIES ◆

Delicious—with a cookie crust and a chewy center—these filled cookies combine two great sources of fiber.

FILLING
1 cup finely chopped dried figs (6 ounces)
⅔ cup orange juice
2 tablespoons clover honey
Pinch of ground cinnamon

DOUGH
⅓ cup nondiet, tub-style safflower- or corn-
    oil margarine
⅔ cup granulated sugar
2 large egg whites
1 teaspoon vanilla extract
1 cup fine oat bran
1⅓ cups all-purpose or unbleached white flour
1½ teaspoons baking powder
⅛ teaspoon salt

To make the filling, combine the figs, orange juice, honey, and cinnamon in a medium-sized saucepan over medium-low heat. Cook, stirring occasionally, until the mixture thickens—about 10 minutes. Reduce the heat slightly if the mixture begins to stick to the bottom of the pan. Cover and refrigerate immediately.

To make the dough, combine the margarine and sugar in a large mixing bowl. Beat with an electric mixer on low speed until well combined and smooth. Add the egg whites and vanilla extract. Beat on medium speed until well combined and smooth.

Combine the oat bran, flour, baking powder, and salt in a medium-sized bowl, and stir to mix well. Add three-fourths of the oat-bran mixture to the margarine-sugar mixture, and beat to mix well. Add the remaining oat-bran mixture and stir in with a large spoon until combined. If necessary, work in the last of the flour with your fingertips. Gather the dough into a ball and cover with plastic wrap. Chill the dough and filling in the refrigerator for 1 to 2 hours.

Preheat the oven to 350° F.

To form cookies, divide the dough in half. With your fingers, press half the dough evenly into the bottom of a nonstick, spray-coated 11¼″ × 7½″ (or slightly larger) baking pan. Spread the cooled filling evenly on top. Roll out the remaining dough between two sheets of wax paper to the size of the baking pan. Cut and patch dough as necessary to make an even rectangle. Peel off the top layer of wax paper. Invert the dough over the filling. Carefully peel off the remaining layer of wax paper. Gently press the dough into place on top of the filling.

Bake for 25 to 30 minutes or until the top crust is slightly browned. Transfer the pan to a wire rack. Immediately cut into squares using a sharp knife. Let stand until warm before removing bars from pan with a wide-bladed spatula.

Makes about 24 squares

◆ DATE BARS ◆

In London, we enjoyed eating date bars from Cranks vegetarian restaurant. Here's our easy-to-make version.

FILLING
3 cups coarsely chopped dried dates (13 ounces)
1½ cups water
1 tablespoon clover honey
Rind of ½ medium-sized lemon, grated (yellow part only)
⅛ teaspoon ground cinnamon

CRUST
⅓ cup packed light brown sugar
⅓ cup nondiet, tub-style safflower- or corn-oil margarine
1 cup enriched all-purpose or unbleached white flour
1¼ cups coarse oat bran
Pinch of ground cinnamon
⅛ teaspoon salt

Preheat the oven to 400° F.

To make the filling, combine the dates, water, honey, lemon rind, and cinnamon in a medium-sized saucepan over medium-low heat. Simmer, stirring occasionally, until the mixture thickens—about 10 minutes. Reduce the heat slightly if the mixture begins to stick to the bottom of the pan. Set aside to cool slightly.

To make the crust, combine the brown sugar and margarine in a large bowl. With two forks, a pastry cutter, or an electric mixer on low speed, work the margarine and brown sugar together until light and fluffy. In a medium-sized bowl combine the flour, oat bran, cinnamon, and salt. Stir to mix well.

Stir the dry ingredients into the sugar-margarine mixture. Mix with a fork or fingers until the mixture resembles coarse meal. Press half the crust mixture into a well-greased or nonstick, spray-coated 13″ × 9″ baking pan. Add the filling, using the back of a large spoon to spread it out evenly over the crust. Top with the remaining crust mixture, spreading it out evenly and pressing it lightly into place over the top of the filling.

Bake for 24 to 29 minutes or until lightly browned. Cool slightly. Cut into bars while still warm.

Makes about 36 2 by 1½-inch bars

◆ APRICOT BARS ◆

Like our date bars, these were inspired by the fruit bars at Cranks vegetarian restaurant in London. They are very tasty and colorful.

FILLING
1¼ cups coarsely chopped dried apricots (6 ounces)
1 large apple, peeled, cored, and shredded or grated
1½ cups water
½ cup granulated sugar
¼ cup clover honey
Generous ⅛ teaspoon ground cinnamon

CRUST
½ cup packed light brown sugar
⅓ cup nondiet, tub-style safflower- or corn-oil margarine
1¼ cups all-purpose or unbleached white flour
1¼ cups coarse oat bran
⅛ teaspoon salt

Preheat the oven to 400° F.

To make the filling, combine the apricots, apple, water, sugar, honey, and cinnamon in a medium-sized saucepan over medium-low heat. Cook, stirring occasionally, until mixture thickens—about 10 minutes. Reduce the heat slightly if the mixture sticks to the bottom of the pan. Set aside to cool slightly.

To make the crust, combine the brown sugar and margarine in a large bowl. With a pastry cutter or an electric mixer on low speed, work the margarine and brown sugar together until light and fluffy. In a medium-sized bowl combine the flour, oat bran, and salt. Stir to mix well.

Stir the dry ingredients into the sugar-margarine mixture. Mix with a fork or fingers until the mixture resembles coarse meal. Press half the crust mixture into a well-greased or nonstick, spray-coated 15" × 11" jelly-roll or similar pan. Add the filling, using the back of a large spoon to spread it out evenly over the crust. Top with the remaining crust mixture, spreading it out evenly and pressing it lightly into place over the top of the filling.

Bake for 22 to 28 minutes or until lightly browned. Cool slightly. Cut into 1½- to 2-inch-long bars while still warm.

Makes 40 to 50 bars

◆ BROWNIES ◆

Chewy and moist.

⅛ teaspoon instant coffee powder or granules
¼ cup nondiet, tub-style safflower- or corn-
  oil margarine
½ cup granulated sugar
⅓ cup unsweetened cocoa powder (not drink mix)
⅓ cup plus 1 tablespoon dark corn syrup
½ cup fine oat bran
2 large egg whites
1½ teaspoons vanilla extract
⅓ cup all-purpose or unbleached white flour
⅛ teaspoon baking soda
⅛ teaspoon salt

Preheat the oven to 350° F.

In a medium-sized saucepan combine the coffee powder, margarine, sugar, cocoa powder, and corn syrup. Heat over medium-low heat, stirring constantly, until the margarine is melted and the ingredients are well combined and smooth. Remove the saucepan from the heat. By hand, stir in the oat bran. Then vigorously stir in the egg whites and vanilla. In a small bowl combine the flour, baking soda, and salt. Stir to mix well. Add the flour mixture to the cocoa mixture, stirring until smooth and well blended.

Spoon the batter into a greased or nonstick, spray-coated 8-inch square baking pan, spreading it out to the pan edges.

Lower the oven temperature to 325° F. Bake for 17 to 20 minutes or until a toothpick inserted in the center comes out clean and the top is almost firm when lightly pressed. Cool pan on a wire rack. Cut into squares.

Makes 16 2-inch squares

7
Crisps, Kuchens, Puddings, and Pie

◆ CRANBERRY-APPLE CRISP ◆

This is crunchy and colorful.

FILLING
3 cups coarsely diced apples, peeled or unpeeled
1 cup whole cranberries, chopped coarse
⅓ cup granulated sugar
2 teaspoons grated orange rind (orange part only)

TOPPING
⅔ cup fine oat bran
⅓ cup all-purpose or unbleached white flour
½ cup packed light brown sugar
¼ cup nondiet, tub-style safflower- or corn-
    oil margarine

Preheat the oven to 350°F.

To make the filling, spread the diced apples and cranberries in the bottom of an 8-inch square baking pan. In a small cup, stir together the sugar and orange rind. Sprinkle the mixture over the apples and cranberries, and stir to coat the fruit.

To make the topping, combine the oat bran, flour, and brown sugar in a medium-sized bowl. Stir to mix well. Blend in the margarine with a fork or fingers until the mixture is crumbly and the margarine is incorporated. Spread the topping over the fruit.

Bake for 35 to 40 minutes or until the topping is crisp and the fruit is cooked through. Serve warm. If desired, top with a small dollop of lowfat frozen vanilla yogurt.

Makes 5 or 6 servings

◆ PEACH CRISP ◆

This dessert is a great way to enjoy juicy, ripe peaches.

FILLING
5 cups peeled and sliced ripe peaches (about 5 to 7
    large)
1 tablespoon all-purpose or unbleached white flour
3 tablespoons granulated sugar
½ teaspoon ground cinnamon

TOPPING
¼ cup all-purpose or unbleached white flour
¼ cup quick-cooking rolled oats
⅓ cup coarse oat bran
¼ cup instant nonfat dry milk powder
½ teaspoon ground cinnamon
½ cup packed light brown sugar
¼ cup nondiet, tub-style safflower- or corn-
    oil margarine

Preheat the oven to 350° F.

To make the filling, spread the peach slices in the bottom of a 9-inch square (or similar) baking pan. Sprinkle with the flour, granulated sugar, and cinnamon. Stir to coat the peaches.

To make the topping, in a medium-sized bowl combine the flour, oats, oat bran, milk powder, cinnamon, brown sugar, and margarine. Blend with a fork or with your fingers until the mixture is crumbly and the margarine is incorporated. Spread the topping over the peaches.

Bake for 25 to 30 minutes or until the top is lightly browned and the filling is bubbly. Serve warm. If desired, top with nonfat frozen vanilla yogurt.

Makes 5 to 7 servings

◆ APPLE CRISP ◆

Our updated version of this old-fashioned favorite is delicious and an excellent source of fiber.

FILLING
7 cups thinly sliced apples, peeled or unpeeled
2 tablespoons granulated sugar
1 teaspoon ground cinnamon

TOPPING
½ cup fine or coarse oat bran
⅓ cup all-purpose or unbleached white flour
½ cup packed light brown sugar
¼ cup nondiet, tub-style safflower- or corn-
oil margarine

Preheat the oven to 350° F.

To make the filling, spread the apple slices in the bottom of a 2-quart casserole or similar baking dish. Sprinkle the apples with the sugar and cinnamon. Stir to coat the apples.

To make the topping, in a medium-sized bowl combine the oat bran, flour, and brown sugar. Stir to mix well. Blend in the margarine with a fork or fingers until the mixture is crumbly and the margarine is incorporated. Spread the topping over the apples. Bake for 35 to 40 minutes or until topping is crisp and apples are cooked. Serve warm, either plain, with milk, or with a dollop of lowfat frozen vanilla yogurt.

Makes 5 or 6 servings

◆ BLUEBERRY-APPLE CRUMBLE ◆

The addition of apples to this tasty fruit dish boosts the fiber and makes the dessert more economical.

¾ cup fine or coarse oat bran
Generous ½ cup packed light or dark brown sugar
⅓ cup instant nonfat dry milk powder
3 tablespoons all-purpose or unbleached white
    flour
1 teaspoon ground cinnamon
3 tablespoons nondiet, tub-style safflower- or corn-
    oil margarine
3 cups peeled and diced Stayman, Rome, or other
    cooking apples
1 tablespoon lemon juice
¼ teaspoon finely grated lemon rind
3 cups fresh or frozen (thawed) unsweetened
    blueberries

Preheat the oven to 375° F.

Stir together the oat bran, brown sugar, milk powder, flour, and cinnamon. Using two forks, cut in the margarine until thoroughly incorporated. (Alternatively, combine the oat bran, brown sugar, milk powder, flour, cinnamon, and margarine in a food processor fitted with a steel blade. Process in on/off pulses until the margarine is incorporated.) Set the mixture aside.

In a large bowl toss the apples with the lemon juice and lemon rind until well combined. Stir in the blueberries. Reserve 1 cup oat-bran mixture for the topping. Add the remaining oat-bran mixture to the fruit, tossing until well mixed. Put the mixture in a 2-quart baking dish. Sprinkle the reserved oat-bran mixture over the top.

Bake for 35 to 40 minutes or until the mixture is bubbly and nicely browned on top and the apples in the center are tender when pierced with a fork. Transfer the baking dish to a cooling rack. The crumble may be served warm or cooled. It is best when fresh but may be stored, refrigerated, for a day or two.

Makes 5 to 7 servings

◆ BROWN BETTY ◆

This easy but tasty recipe is a great way to use up bread that's drying out. Use our Oatmeal Bread (see Index) or a commercial oat-bran bread. Microwave directions are also provided. We like Brown Betty best made with tart cooking apples such as Granny Smith.

4 cups peeled, diced apples
3 cups ¼- to ½-inch bread cubes made from oat-
    bran bread
½ cup packed light brown sugar
2 tablespoons nondiet, tub-style safflower- or corn-
    oil margarine
½ teaspoon ground cinnamon
⅓ cup hot water

Preheat the oven to 375° F.

Spread half of the apples in the bottom of a greased or nonstick, spray-coated 2-quart (or similar-sized) baking dish with a cover. Spread half of the bread cubes over the apples, and then cover with half of the brown sugar. Dot with half of the margarine and sprinkle with half of the cinnamon. Repeat with another layer of apples, bread cubes, brown sugar, margarine, and cinnamon. Pour the water evenly over the top.

Cover and bake 35 to 40 minutes or until the apples are almost cooked through. Uncover and bake an additional 10 to 12 minutes or until the pudding is slightly browned on top.

Microwave Directions: Prepare the Betty as above. Cover the baking dish with wax paper. Microwave on high power 7 to 9 minutes, turning the dish one-quarter turn twice during the cooking period. Uncover and microwave an additional 3 to 4 minutes on high power, turning one-quarter turn once during the cooking period. The top will not be browned.

Serve warm. Top with a small dollop of nonfat frozen yogurt if desired.

Makes 4 to 6 servings

◆ PEACH COBBLER ◆

An easy biscuit crust over canned peaches makes for a quick dessert.

FILLING
1 29-ounce can juice-packed sliced peaches
2 tablespoons granulated sugar
¼ teaspoon ground cinnamon

TOPPING
½ cup fine oat bran
½ cup plus 1 tablespoon all-purpose or unbleached
    white flour
3 tablespoons granulated sugar
1 teaspoon baking powder
¼ teaspoon baking soda
⅛ teaspoon salt
3 tablespoons nondiet, tub-style safflower- or corn-
    oil margarine
½ cup commercial buttermilk

Preheat the oven to 400° F.

To make the filling, drain the peaches and reserve the juice. Arrange the peach slices in the bottom of an 8-inch square baking pan. Pour 2 tablespoons of the juice over the peaches. Mix together the sugar and cinnamon. Sprinkle over the peaches.

To make the topping, combine the oat bran, flour, sugar, baking powder, baking soda, and salt in a medium-sized bowl. Stir to mix well. Cut in the margarine with a pastry cutter, fork, or fingers until mixture resembles coarse meal. With a large spoon, stir in the buttermilk.

Drop large spoonfuls of the topping over the filling mixture, and spread out with the back of the spoon. The topping need not completely cover the filling. Bake for 25 to 30 minutes or until the dough is cooked through and is very lightly browned. Let the cobbler sit for 5 to 10 minutes before serving. Serve warm. If desired, top with lowfat frozen yogurt.

Makes 4 or 5 servings

◆ MICROWAVE PEACH KUCHEN ◆

Canned peaches make this easy recipe extra convenient. Serve this as a breakfast treat or snack.

> 1 16-ounce can juice-packed sliced peaches
> 3 tablespoons nondiet, tub-style safflower- or corn-
>   oil margarine
> 1 teaspoon vanilla extract
> ⅓ cup granulated sugar
> 2 egg whites
> ½ cup all-purpose or unbleached white flour
> ½ cup fine oat bran
> 1 teaspoon baking powder
> ⅛ teaspoon salt
> ⅓ cup commercial buttermilk
> 2 tablespoons packed light brown sugar for topping

Set the peaches aside in a colander or sieve until thoroughly drained.

In a large mixing bowl with an electric mixer on medium speed, beat together the margarine, vanilla, and sugar. Beat in the egg whites. In a separate bowl stir together the flour, oat bran, baking powder, and salt. Add the flour mixture and the buttermilk to the margarine mixture, beating until blended. Stir the peaches into the batter.

Pour batter into an 8-inch round and at least 2-inch deep (or similar-sized) greased or nonstick, spray-coated glass baking dish. Rap dish against countertop to remove any large air bubbles. Cover the dish with wax paper. Microwave on 70 percent power for 5½ to 6½ minutes, rotating the dish one-quarter turn twice during the cooking period. Rotate one-quarter turn, and microwave on 100 percent power for 3½ to 4½ minutes or until the kuchen top springs back when lightly pressed and a toothpick inserted in the center comes out clean.

Sprinkle the brown sugar evenly over the kuchen top. Replace the wax paper. Microwave 50 to 60 seconds on high power until the brown sugar has melted. Remove the baking dish to a wire rack, and let the kuchen stand for 5 minutes. Serve warm. Cut the kuchen into wedges, and carefully remove them using a spatula or cake knife. Or spoon out portions.

Makes 5 to 7 servings

◆ PLUM KUCHEN ◆

Plum kuchen is as appealing and delicious as a fruit tart but far lower in fat and cholesterol. It is good made with a wide variety of plums, particularly those with full flavor and a sweet-tart tang.

DOUGH
⅔ cup fine oat bran
1 large egg white
⅓ cup plain nonfat yogurt
1½ teaspoons vanilla extract
¾ cup all-purpose or unbleached white flour
½ cup granulated sugar
½ teaspoon baking powder
¼ cup nondiet, tub-style safflower- or corn-
    oil margarine

FRUIT AND TOPPING
1¼ pounds ripe plums (about 6 to 7 medium-
    sized), pitted and cut into eighths
3 tablespoons granulated sugar combined with ¾
    teaspoon ground cinnamon

Preheat the oven to 400°F.

In a medium-sized bowl mix together the oat bran, egg white, yogurt, and vanilla until thoroughly blended. Set aside for 5 minutes.

Thoroughly stir together the flour, sugar, and baking powder. Add the margarine to the flour mixture. Using a pastry blender or two forks, cut in the margarine until the mixture resembles coarse meal. Using a large wooden spoon, stir the flour mixture into the yogurt mixture until thoroughly blended but not overmixed; the dough will be stiff.

Spoon the mixture into a greased or nonstick, spray-coated 10-inch (or similar) springform pan or pie plate. Using a lightly greased table knife, spread out the dough to form a smooth, evenly thick layer, or if preferred, lay a sheet of wax paper over the dough and press it out into a smooth layer. Arrange the plum slices, one cut-side down and just touching, in an attractive concentric-circle pattern on the dough; lightly press slices down to imbed slightly. Sprinkle the topping mixture evenly over the plums.

Bake for 28 to 33 minutes or until the top is bubbly and the plums are cooked through. Transfer the kuchen to a rack and let stand until completely cooled. If a springform pan was used, run a small knife around the kuchen and release the pan sides. Then serve the kuchen from a large round plate, cut into wedges. If a pie plate was used, the kuchen can be served directly from the plate, cut into wedges.

Makes 7 to 9 servings

Note: If the plums are tart or not fully ripe, add 1 or 2 extra tablespoons of granulated sugar to the topping mixture.

◆ CHERRY PUDDING CAKE ◆

An easy-to-make batter is poured over a zesty sour-cherry sauce and baked until puffy and golden. Extra sauce is spooned over the cake at serving time.

SAUCE AND CHERRIES
½ cup granulated sugar
2½ tablespoons cornstarch
1½ cups cranberry-juice cocktail or cranapple juice
1 16-ounce can pitted tart red (pie) cherries,
    including juice
2 teaspoons lemon juice
Pinch of very finely grated lemon rind (yellow part
    only)
Pinch of ground cinnamon

CAKE
¾ cup fine oat bran
1 large egg white
½ cup plus 1 tablespoon plain nonfat yogurt
1½ teaspoons vanilla extract
⅛ teaspoon finely grated lemon rind (yellow part
    only)
⅔ cup all-purpose or unbleached white flour
⅓ cup granulated sugar
¼ teaspoon baking powder
¼ teaspoon baking soda
3 tablespoons nondiet, tub-style safflower- or corn-
    oil margarine

Preheat the oven to 375° F.

To prepare the sauce, thoroughly stir together the sugar and cornstarch in a medium-sized saucepan. Slowly stir in the cranberry-juice cocktail until well blended and smooth. Drain *all* the juice from the cherries into a measuring cup. (Reserve the cherries for the cake.) Add the lemon juice, lemon rind, and cinnamon to the cherry juice. If necessary, add enough water to the mixture to yield 1 cup of liquid. Stir the liquid into the sugar-cornstarch mixture. Heat the mixture over high heat, stirring, until it bubbles and thickens slightly and becomes clear. Remove the mixture from the heat. Measure out $1\frac{1}{2}$ cups cherry sauce and pour into a lightly greased $2\frac{1}{2}$-quart (or larger) casserole or deep-sided baking dish. Reserve the remaining sauce for serving over the pudding cake.

To prepare the cake, mix together the oat bran, egg white, yogurt, vanilla, and lemon rind in a medium-sized bowl until thoroughly blended. Set aside for 5 minutes to allow oat bran to absorb some of the liquid.

Thoroughly stir together the flour, sugar, baking powder, and baking soda. Add the margarine to the flour mixture. Using a pastry blender or two forks, cut in the margarine until the mixture resembles coarse meal. Stir the flour mixture into the yogurt mixture until thoroughly blended but not overmixed. Fold in the cherries. Spoon the batter evenly over the sauce mixture in the casserole; *do not attempt to stir or spread out the batter.*

Bake in the preheated oven for 25 to 35 minutes or until the top is nicely browned and puffy and a toothpick inserted in the thickest part comes out clean. The pudding cake is best served slightly warm and should be eaten within a day or two. Serve the extra cherry sauce separately in a sauceboat, or spoon a bit of it over each serving.

Makes 5 to 7 servings

◆ CHOCOLATE BREAD PUDDING ◆

This good and easy pudding can be made from leftover cubes of Oatmeal Bread (see Index), English Muffin Bread (see Index), or a commercial oatmeal or oat-bran bread.

  ½ cup fine oat bran
  ⅓ cup unsweetened cocoa powder (not drink mix)
  ¾ cup packed brown sugar
  Pinch of ground cinnamon
  Pinch of ground nutmeg
  3½ cups skim milk
  1 tablespoon nondiet, tub-style safflower- or corn-
    oil margarine
  1½ teaspoons vanilla extract
  2¼ cups ¼- to ½-inch cubes of oatmeal (or oat-
    bran) bread

Preheat the oven to 375° F.

In a medium-sized saucepan thoroughly stir together the oat bran, cocoa powder, brown sugar, cinnamon, and nutmeg. Gradually add 1½ cups of the milk, stirring until well blended. Place the pan over medium heat and cook, stirring, until mixture comes to a boil. Boil for 30 seconds, stirring constantly to prevent sticking. Stir in the remaining 2 cups of milk and reheat the mixture, stirring, until hot but not boiling. Remove from the heat and stir in the margarine and vanilla. Set aside.

Spread the bread cubes in a lightly greased or nonstick, spray-coated 2-quart (or slightly larger) casserole. Pour the cocoa mixture over the bread, being sure to moisten all the cubes.

Reset the oven to 350° F, and bake the pudding for 35 to 45 minutes or until nicely browned and puffy on top. Transfer the casserole to a wire rack and let stand at least 10 minutes before serving. The pudding is best served warm and may be reheated, if desired. It should be stored in the refrigerator and will keep for a day or so.

Makes 6 to 8 servings

◆ FRENCH APPLE PIE ◆

Juicy and not too sweet, this apple pie always gets rave reviews.

CRUST
¾ cup all-purpose or unbleached white flour
½ cup fine oat bran
¼ teaspoon salt
¼ cup safflower or corn oil
2½ tablespoons skim milk

FILLING
6 cups thinly sliced, peeled, tart apples (about 5
   large)
Scant ⅔ cup granulated sugar
3 tablespoons all-purpose or unbleached white
   flour
½ teaspoon ground cinnamon

TOPPING
⅓ cup fine oat bran
¼ cup all-purpose or unbleached white flour
⅓ cup packed light brown sugar
3 tablespoons nondiet, tub-style safflower- or corn-
   oil margarine

To make the crust, stir the flour, oat bran, and salt together in the bottom of a 9-inch pie plate. With a fork, beat the oil and milk together until mixed well. Slowly add the oil-milk mixture to the oat-bran mixture, stirring vigorously with a fork. With your fingers, work in the oil-milk mixture until the oat-bran mixture is moistened and holds together. (If all the oil-milk mixture is incorporated and the dough is still a bit dry, add a few extra drops of milk. However, be careful not to overmoisten.) Gather the dough into a ball. Then, with your fingers, press into place in the pie plate, working the dough out thinly and evenly over the bottom and up the sides. Crimp the pastry rim with your fingers or press into place with the tines of a fork. Cover the unbaked crust with plastic wrap and refrigerate for at least 1 hour and up to 8 hours before using, to allow dough to "relax" and become more tender.

Preheat the oven to 400° F.

To make the filling, combine the apples, sugar, flour, and cinnamon in a large bowl. Stir to mix well. Arrange the apple mixture evenly on top of the chilled crust.

To make the topping, combine the oat bran, flour, and brown sugar in a medium-sized bowl. Mix well with a fork or fingers. Blend in the margarine with a fork or fingers until completely incorporated. Spread the topping over the apples.

To prevent the crust from becoming too brown, cover the edges with a 3-inch-wide strip of aluminum foil, folding the foil to the underside of the pie-plate rim. Do not remove the foil during baking. Additionally, during the last 15 to 20 minutes of baking, cover the top of the pie with a sheet of aluminum foil to prevent the topping from browning too much.

Bake for 55 to 60 minutes or until the apples are tender when pierced with a fork and the filling is bubbly.

Makes 6 to 8 servings

Note: For a pie with slightly less sugar and slightly more oat bran, the proportions in the topping can be changed as follows:

> ⅓ cup plus 2 tablespoons fine oat bran
> ¼ cup all-purpose or unbleached white flour
> ¼ cup packed light brown sugar
> 3 tablespoons nondiet, tub-style safflower- or corn-oil margarine

8
Breakfast Cereals and Pancakes

◆ GRANOLA ◆

For a larger batch, simply double this easy recipe and bake in two pans.

3½ cups quick-cooking or old-fashioned rolled oats
2 cups coarse or fine oat bran
2 tablespoons instant nonfat dry milk powder
½ cup clover or other mild honey
⅓ cup safflower or corn oil
Optional: 1 to 1½ cups dried fruit (seedless
     raisins, chopped apricots, or any desired
     combination of chopped mixed fruit)

Preheat the oven to 250° F.

In a large bowl combine the rolled oats, oat bran, and milk powder. Stir to mix well. Combine the honey and oil in a large nonmetal measuring cup or small bowl, and microwave on high heat for 50 to 60 seconds. (Alternatively, heat the honey and oil in a small saucepan over medium heat, stirring to blend.) When the honey-oil mixture is blended and fluid, pour it over the dry ingredients, stirring. Stir 1 or 2 minutes, until the dry mixture is well coated.

Spread the mixture in a nonstick, spray-coated 11″ × 15″ jelly-roll (or similar) pan. With the back of a large spoon, press the mixture lightly into the pan. Bake for 60 to 70 minutes, stirring two or three times, until the granola is lightly browned and tastes cooked. The granola will become much crunchier as it cools.

Transfer the pan to a wire rack, stir in the dried fruit (if used), and cool. When the granola is thoroughly cooled, store in refrigerator in an airtight container or plastic bag.

Makes 5½ to 7 cups

◆ MOLASSES GRANOLA ◆

Molasses gives this granola a distinctive flavor. For a larger batch, simply double the recipe and bake in two pans.

> 3 cups quick-cooking or old-fashioned rolled oats
> 2½ cups coarse or fine oat bran
> 3 tablespoons instant nonfat dry milk powder
> Generous ½ cup light molasses
> ⅓ cup safflower or corn oil
> 1 cup dark seedless raisins

Preheat the oven to 250° F.

In a large bowl combine the rolled oats, oat bran, and milk powder. Stir to mix well. Stir together the molasses and oil in a large measuring cup or small bowl and microwave on high heat for 50 to 60 seconds. (Alternatively, heat the molasses and oil in a small saucepan over medium heat, stirring to blend.) When the molasses-oil mixture is blended and fluid, pour it over the dry ingredients, stirring. Stir 1 or 2 minutes, until the dry mixture is well coated.

Spread the mixture in a nonstick, spray-coated 11″ × 15″ jelly-roll (or similar) pan. With the back of a large spoon, lightly press the mixture into the pan. Bake in the preheated oven for 60 to 70 minutes, stirring two or three times, until the granola is lightly browned and tastes cooked. The granola will become much crunchier as it cools.

Transfer the pan to a wire rack, stir in the raisins, and cool. When the granola is thoroughly cooled, store in the refrigerator in an airtight container or plastic bag.

Makes 6½ cups

◆ MUESLI CEREAL ◆

For a larger batch of muesli, this recipe can easily be doubled. Bake the double batch in two pans.

4 cups old-fashioned or quick-cooking rolled oats
2 cups fine or coarse oat bran
¼ cup sesame seeds
¼ cup instant nonfat dry milk powder
⅓ cup clover or other mild honey
¼ cup corn or safflower oil
½ cup dark seedless raisins

Preheat the oven to 250° F.

In a large bowl combine the rolled oats, oat bran, sesame seeds, and milk powder. Stir to mix well. Combine the honey and oil in a large nonmetal measuring cup or small bowl, and microwave on high heat for 50 to 60 seconds. (Alternatively, heat the honey and oil in a small saucepan over medium heat, stirring to blend.) When the honey-oil mixture is blended and fluid, pour it over the dry ingredients, stirring. Stir 1 or 2 minutes, until the dry mixture is well coated.

Spread the mixture in a nonstick, spray-coated 12″ × 15″ jelly-roll (or similar) pan. Bake for 50 to 60 minutes, stirring two or three times, until the muesli is browned and crunchy. Transfer the pan to a wire rack, stir in the raisins, and cool. When the muesli is cooled, store it in the refrigerator in an airtight container or plastic bag.

Makes about 6 cups

◆ MIXED-GRAIN PANCAKES ◆

Cornmeal gives these pancakes a pleasantly different flavor and texture.

¾ cup all-purpose or unbleached white flour
½ cup fine oat bran
½ cup white or yellow cornmeal
¼ cup quick-cooking rolled oats
1 tablespoon granulated sugar
1 teaspoon baking powder
½ teaspoon baking soda
⅛ teaspoon salt
1 large egg white
3 tablespoons safflower or corn oil
1½ cups commercial buttermilk

In a large bowl combine the flour, oat bran, cornmeal, oats, sugar, baking powder, baking soda, and salt, and stir to mix well. Add the egg white, oil, and buttermilk, and stir until batter is smooth. The batter will be fairly thick.

Cook the pancakes at medium heat on a preheated, seasoned griddle or skillet that has been very lightly greased with oil or a nonstick spray coating. Or use a nonstick griddle.

Form each pancake by ladling ¼ cup of the batter onto the griddle. Shake the griddle back and forth several times to spread the batter out into a 3½- to 4-inch circle. Cook the pancakes until browned on the bottom. Turn each pancake with a spatula, and cook until the other side is nicely browned and the pancake is cooked through.

If the batter thickens upon standing, stir in some more buttermilk.

If necessary, re-oil the griddle by brushing it lightly with a paper towel moistened with oil.

Makes 14 to 15 medium-sized pancakes

◆ HOMEMADE PANCAKE MIX ◆

This makes a generous 4 cups of low-cholesterol dry pancake or quick-bread mix. Each cup of mix yields 6 to 8 3- to 4-inch pancakes (see the recipe for Buttermilk Pancakes that follows). The mix can also be used to make Quick Raisin Muffins and Streusel Coffee Cake (see Index). Store the mix on a pantry shelf for up to a month; keep it in the refrigerator if storing longer.

2 cups all-purpose or unbleached white flour
¾ cup whole-wheat flour
1¼ cups fine oat bran
⅓ cup instant nonfat dry milk powder
Generous ¾ teaspoon salt
2 tablespoons baking powder
¾ teaspoon baking soda

Stir together the white flour, whole-wheat flour, oat bran, milk powder, salt, baking powder, and baking soda until very well blended. Store in an airtight container in a cool place.

Makes 4 generous cups of mix

◆ BUTTERMILK PANCAKES ◆

These pancakes may be made with or without egg white. Pancakes without egg white tend to become rubbery as they cool but have a satisfactory texture if eaten hot off the griddle.

This recipe makes 6 to 8 pancakes but may be doubled, tripled, etc. Fresh or thawed frozen blueberries may be added to batter, if desired.

1 cup Homemade Pancake Mix (see preceding
   recipe)
1 tablespoon oil
1 egg white (optional)
1 to 1¼ cups commercial buttermilk
½ cup fresh or frozen (thawed) blueberries
   (optional)

Stir together the pancake mix, oil, and egg white (if used) in a medium-sized bowl. Gradually stir in enough buttermilk to yield a rather thick batter (about the consistency of sour cream). Gently fold in the blueberries (if used). If batter thickens upon standing, stir in a little more buttermilk until the desired consistency is obtained.

Cook the pancakes on a preheated, seasoned griddle or skillet that has been very lightly brushed with oil or coated with a nonstick spray and placed over medium heat. For each pancake spoon about 2½ tablespoons of batter onto the griddle and cook over medium heat for about 30 to 40 seconds. Turn over pancakes using a spatula, and continue cooking until nicely browned and cooked through. Serve the pancakes while still hot.

Makes 6 to 8 medium-sized pancakes

9
Crackers

◆ ONION CRISPS ◆

These crisp, flavorful crackers have the texture of wheat thins.

1¼ cups coarse oat bran
¾ cup all-purpose or unbleached white flour
2 tablespoons instant (dried) minced onion
½ teaspoon baking soda
Scant ⅛ teaspoon garlic powder
Generous ½ teaspoon salt
2 tablespoons safflower, corn, or olive oil
Scant ⅔ cup commercial buttermilk
2 to 3 drops Tabasco sauce

Preheat the oven to 350° F.

In a medium-sized bowl combine the oat bran, flour, onion, baking soda, garlic powder, and salt. Stir to mix well. Add the oil, buttermilk, and Tabasco sauce, and stir with a large spoon until thoroughly combined. If necessary, work in the last of the flour with your fingertips. If the dough seems crumbly, add a teaspoon or two more buttermilk. Gather the dough into a ball.

Let the dough rest, uncovered, for 10 to 12 minutes, until it becomes less sticky. To form each cracker, roll a generous ½ teaspoon of dough into a ball. Place the ball on a very well-greased or nonstick, spray-coated baking sheet. Cover with wax paper. Use the bottom of a drinking glass to flatten the dough into a 2-inch round. Remove wax paper. Repeat until all the crackers are formed.

Bake the rounds for 8 to 11 minutes or until browned at the edges and crisp. Remove immediately from baking sheet with a metal spatula. Cool completely on a wire rack. Then store in an airtight container.

Makes 50 to 60 crackers

◆ PIZZA CRACKERS ◆

It's surprising how little cheese it takes to give these crackers a pizza tang. The dough may be shaped into round or rectangular crackers.

> ¾ cup plus 2 tablespoons all-purpose or
>   unbleached white flour
> ¾ cup coarse or fine oat bran
> 1 tablespoon grated Parmesan cheese
> 2 teaspoons instant (dried) minced onion
> ½ teaspoon baking soda
> ½ teaspoon dried basil leaves
> ¼ teaspoon dried oregano leaves
> ⅛ teaspoon dried thyme leaves
> ⅛ teaspoon garlic powder
> ¼ teaspoon salt
> ⅛ teaspoon black pepper
> 2 tablespoons olive, safflower, or corn oil
> Scant ½ cup canned tomato sauce

Preheat the oven to 350° F.

In a medium-sized bowl combine the flour, oat bran, cheese, onion, baking soda, basil, oregano, thyme, garlic powder, salt, and pepper. Stir to mix well. Add the oil and tomato sauce, and stir with a large spoon until thoroughly combined. If necessary, work in the last of the flour with your fingertips. If the dough is crumbly, add about a teaspoon more tomato sauce or enough to make the dough cohesive.

For round crackers, allow the dough to rest, uncovered, for 10 or 12 minutes, until it is less sticky. To form each cracker, roll a generous ½ teaspoon of dough into a ball. Place the ball on a very well-greased or nonstick, spray-coated baking sheet. Cover with wax paper. Flatten each ball of dough into a 2-inch round with the bottom of a drinking glass, using a circular, rocking motion. Remove wax paper. Repeat until all the crackers are formed. Bake the rounds for 8 to 11 minutes or until orange-colored and crisp. Remove immediately from the baking sheet with a metal spatula. Cool on a wire rack.

For rectangular crackers, allow the dough to rest 5 to 6 minutes uncovered. Then divide the dough in half and form each half into a large ball. (Cover the second dough ball with plastic wrap while working with the first.)

Roll out one large dough ball *directly* on a greased or nonstick, spray-coated baking sheet that has at least two rimless edges (or directly on the *back* of a large baking sheet with sides). Place a sheet of wax paper on top of the dough. Roll out to a 9- or 10- by 11-inch rectangle. Try to keep the thickness of the dough as even as possible, as thick crackers will not be as crisp. Cut and patch the dough as necessary to make the sides of the rectangle straight. Gently peel off and discard the wax paper immediately after rolling out the dough.

Use a sharp knife, pizza cutter, or pastry wheel to cut the rolled-out dough into squares about $1\frac{1}{2}$ to 2 inches on a side, *leaving the dough in place* on the baking sheets or pan bottoms. Or cut squares in half to form triangles. Prick dough all over with a fork. Repeat the rolling and cutting procedure with the second portion of dough.

Bake for 12 to 15 minutes or until the crackers on the edges of the sheets are lightly browned and crisp. Remove the baking sheets from the oven, and separate the browned crackers from the rest of the sheet with a metal spatula. Transfer the browned crackers to a wire rack to cool, and return the baking sheets to the oven. Continue baking, checking the crackers about every $1\frac{1}{2}$ to 2 minutes and removing them from the sheets as they are done. Continue until all the crackers are done. When the crackers are slightly cooled, separate any that are still stuck together.

Cool on the wire rack. When completely cooled, store in an airtight container.

Makes 50 round crackers or 40 to 50 rectangular crackers

◆ VEGETABLE CRACKERS ◆

The flavors of tomato, celery, and dill predominate in these zesty crackers.

1¼ cups fine or coarse oat bran
1 cup all-purpose or unbleached white flour
¼ cup instant nonfat dry milk powder
2 teaspoons granulated sugar
¼ teaspoon baking soda
1 tablespoon instant (dried) minced onion
¼ teaspoon salt
¼ teaspoon celery salt
¼ teaspoon chili powder
¼ teaspoon dill
⅛ teaspoon black pepper
2½ tablespoons corn, safflower, or olive oil
½ cup tomato sauce

Preheat the oven to 350°F.

In a medium-sized bowl stir together the oat bran, flour, milk powder, sugar, baking soda, onion, salt, celery salt, chili powder, dill, and black pepper. Add the oil and tomato sauce, and stir until well mixed. If mixture is too crumbly to hold together, stir in a little water, a teaspoon at a time, until the dough becomes cohesive. Knead the dough in the bowl five or six times, until it is very smooth.

Divide the dough in half. Form each half into a ball. Center each half on a lightly greased or nonstick, spray-coated baking sheet with at least two rimless edges (or use the *back* of a large rimmed baking pan). Lay a sheet of wax paper over each portion of dough. Roll out one portion into a 10- by 12-inch rectangle, keeping the thickness of the dough as even as possible. Carefully peel off the wax paper, and cut and patch the dough as necessary to form the rectangle. Prick the dough all over using a fork. Then, using a large, sharp knife, pizza cutter, or pastry wheel and working directly on the baking sheet, cut the dough horizontally at approximately 1½-inch intervals and vertically at 1-inch intervals; *leave the dough in place on the baking sheet.* Repeat the rolling and cutting procedure with the second portion of dough.

Bake in the preheated oven for 13 to 15 minutes or until the crackers on the edges of the sheets are lightly browned and crisp. Remove the baking sheets from the oven, and separate the browned crackers from the rest of the sheet with a metal spatula. Transfer the browned crackers to a wire rack to cool, and return the baking sheets to the oven. Continue baking, checking the crackers about every 2 minutes and removing them from the sheets as they are done. Continue until all the crackers are done. Let the crackers stand until cooled slightly. Separate the ones that are still stuck together with your fingers. Cool the crackers thoroughly, and immediately pack in an airtight container.

Makes 80 to 90 1½- by 1- inch crackers

◆ HERB CRACKERS ◆

Try these with soup or by themselves as a snack.

1 cup all-purpose or unbleached white flour
¾ cup coarse oat bran
2 teaspoons instant (dried) minced onion
½ teaspoon baking soda
½ teaspoon dried thyme leaves
½ teaspoon dried basil leaves
½ teaspoon salt
⅛ teaspoon garlic powder
⅛ teaspoon ground white pepper
2 tablespoons safflower, corn, or olive oil
½ cup commercial buttermilk

Preheat the oven to 350°F.

In a medium-sized bowl combine the flour, oat bran, onion, baking soda, thyme, basil, salt, garlic powder, and white pepper. Stir to mix well. Add the oil and buttermilk, and stir with a large spoon until thoroughly combined. If necessary, work in the last of the flour with your fingertips. With your fingers, gather dough into a ball.

Divide dough in half and form each half into a ball. (Cover second ball with plastic wrap while working with first.)

Roll out one dough ball *directly* on a greased or nonstick, spray-coated sheet that has at least two rimless edges (or directly on the *back* of a large baking sheet with sides). Place a sheet of wax paper on top of the dough. Roll out the dough to a 9- or 10- by 11-inch rectangle. Try to keep the thickness of the dough as even as possible, as thick crackers will not be as crisp. Cut and patch the dough as necessary to make the sides of the rectangle straight. Gently peel off and discard the wax paper immediately after rolling out the dough.

Prick the dough all over with a fork. Then use a sharp knife, pizza cutter, or pastry wheel to cut the rolled-out dough into squares about 1½ to 2 inches on a side, *leaving the dough in place* on the baking sheet or pan bottom. If desired, cut the squares into triangles. Repeat for the second dough ball.

Bake for 12 to 15 minutes or until the crackers on the edges of the sheets are lightly browned and crisp. Remove the baking sheets from the oven, and separate the browned crackers from the rest of the sheet with a metal spatula. Transfer the browned crackers to a wire rack to cool, and return the baking sheets to the oven. Continue baking, checking the crackers about every 1½ to 2 minutes and removing them from the sheets as they are done. Continue until all the crackers are done. When the crackers are slightly cooled, separate any that are still stuck together.

Cool completely on the wire rack. Then store in an airtight container.

Makes 50 to 60 crackers

◆ SAVORY CRACKERS ◆

Crunchy and flavorful, these crackers are great served alone, without any of the usual fattening accompaniments.

1 cup coarse oat bran
¾ cup all-purpose or unbleached white flour
2 teaspoons instant (dried) minced onion
½ teaspoon baking soda
½ teaspoon chili powder
Scant ⅛ teaspoon garlic powder
⅛ teaspoon paprika
⅛ teaspoon cayenne pepper
¼ teaspoon salt
2 tablespoons safflower, corn, or olive oil
½ cup commercial buttermilk
¼ teaspoon salt for topping (optional)

Preheat the oven to 350° F.

In a medium-sized bowl combine the oat bran, flour, onion, baking soda, chili powder, garlic powder, paprika, cayenne pepper, and salt. Stir to mix well. Add the oil and buttermilk, and stir with a large spoon until thoroughly combined. If necessary, work in the last of the flour with your fingertips. If the dough seems crumbly, add a bit more buttermilk. Let the dough rest, uncovered, for 4 or 5 minutes.

Divide the dough in half and form each half into a ball. (Cover the second dough ball with plastic wrap while working with the first.)

Roll out one dough ball *directly* on a greased or nonstick, spray-coated baking sheet that has at least two rimless edges (or directly on the *back* of a large baking sheet with sides). Place a sheet of wax paper on top of the dough. Roll out the dough to a 9- or 10- by 12-inch rectangle. Try to keep the thickness of the dough as even as possible, as thick crackers will not be as crisp. Cut and patch dough as necessary to make the sides of the rectangle straight. Gently peel off and discard the wax paper immediately after rolling out the dough.

Prick the dough all over with a fork. Then use a sharp knife, pizza cutter, or pastry wheel to cut the rolled-out dough into squares about 1½ to 2 inches on a side, *leaving the dough in place* on the baking sheet or pan bottom. If desired, cut the squares into triangles.

Repeat for the second dough ball. If desired, sprinkle the crackers with an additional ¼ teaspoon salt.

Bake for 12 to 15 minutes or until the crackers on the edges of the sheets are lightly browned and crisp. Remove the baking sheets from the oven, and separate the browned crackers from the rest of the sheet with a metal spatula. Transfer the browned crackers to a wire rack to cool, and return the baking sheets to the oven. Continue baking, checking the crackers about every 1½ to 2 minutes and removing them from the sheets as they are done. Continue until all the crackers are done. When the crackers are slightly cooled, separate any that are still stuck together.

Cool completely on the wire rack. Then store in an airtight container.

Makes 45 to 50 crackers

◆ CORN-SESAME WAFERS ◆

These thin crackers have an appealing crispness and a light corn-and-oat taste.

1 cup fine or coarse oat bran
½ cup yellow cornmeal
½ cup all-purpose or unbleached white flour
1 tablespoon granulated sugar
Generous ½ teaspoon salt
¼ teaspoon baking soda
2½ tablespoons safflower, corn, or olive oil
Approximately ½ cup commercial buttermilk
2 tablespoons sesame seeds

Preheat the oven to 375° F.

Thoroughly stir together the oat bran, cornmeal, flour, sugar, all except ⅛ teaspoon of the salt, and baking soda in a medium-sized bowl. Stir in the oil and buttermilk. Let the mixture stand for 3 to 4 minutes. If the mixture seems dry and crumbly, gradually stir in just enough more buttermilk for the dough to hold together (but not become wet or soggy). Knead the dough in the bowl seven or eight times, until smooth and cohesive.

To form wafers, pull off portions of the dough and shape them into generous 1-inch balls. Space the balls about 2½ inches apart on greased baking sheets. Working with one ball of dough at a time, cover with a sheet of wax paper, and flatten by pressing down on the ball with the bottom of a flat-bottomed drinking glass until the dough is about 2 inches in diameter. Remove wax paper. Continue until all the wafers are formed. Sprinkle the rounds lightly with sesame seeds and then the reserved ⅛ teaspoon salt. Lay the wax paper over the wafers, and pat down to imbed the seeds slightly.

Bake the wafers for 9 to 12 minutes or until they are nicely tinged with brown around the edges and crisp. Remove the sheets from the oven and, using a spatula, carefully transfer the wafers to wire racks and let stand until completely cooled. Store in an airtight container for up to a week.

Makes about 30 to 35 2½-inch wafers

◆ CHILI CORN THINS ◆

¾ cup yellow cornmeal
¾ cup coarse oat bran
1 teaspoon chili powder
½ teaspoon baking soda
½ teaspoon salt
⅛ teaspoon cayenne pepper
Scant ½ cup commercial buttermilk
2 tablespoons safflower, corn, or olive oil

Preheat the oven to 350° F.

In a medium-sized bowl combine the cornmeal, oat bran, chili powder, baking soda, salt, and cayenne pepper. Stir to mix well. Add the buttermilk and oil, and mix with a large spoon until the dough is completely moistened. If the dough seems crumbly, add a bit more buttermilk. Use your fingers to knead the dough a few times until smooth.

Roll out the dough *directly* on a greased or nonstick, spray-coated baking sheet that has at least two rimless edges (or directly on the *back* of a large baking sheet with sides). Place a sheet of wax paper on top of the dough. Roll out the dough to an 11- or 12- by 15½-inch rectangle. Try to keep the thickness of the dough as even as possible, as thick crackers will not be as crisp. Cut and patch the dough as necessary to make the sides of the rectangle straight. Gently peel off and discard the wax paper immediately after rolling out the dough.

With a sharp knife or pizza cutter, cut the rolled-out dough into small (about 1-inch by ¾-inch) rectangles. *Leave the dough in place* on the baking sheet or pan bottom. Prick dough all over using a fork.

Bake for 13 to 16 minutes or until the crackers on the edges of the sheet are lightly browned and crisp. Remove sheet from oven, and separate the browned crackers from the rest of the sheet with a metal spatula. Transfer the browned crackers to a wire rack to cool, and return baking sheet to oven. Continue baking, checking the crackers about every 1½ to 2 minutes and removing them from the sheet as they are done. Continue until all the crackers are done. When the crackers are slightly cooled, separate any that are still stuck together.

Cool on a wire rack. Then store in an airtight container.

Makes about 100 corn thins

◆ RYE ROUNDS ◆

Vary the amount of caraway seeds in these crackers according to taste.

1¼ cups coarse oat bran
¾ cup medium rye flour
2 teaspoons instant (dried) minced onion
1½ teaspoons granulated sugar
1 to 1½ teaspoons caraway seeds
½ teaspoon baking soda
Scant ⅛ teaspoon garlic powder
Generous ½ teaspoon salt
3 tablespoons olive, safflower, or corn oil
Scant ½ cup commercial buttermilk

Preheat the oven to 350° F.

In a medium-sized bowl combine the oat bran, rye flour, onion, sugar, caraway seeds, baking soda, garlic powder, and salt. Stir to mix well. Add the oil and buttermilk, and stir with a large spoon until thoroughly combined. If necessary, work in the last of the flour with your fingertips. The dough should be fairly moist and come together in a ball. If it is crumbly, add 1 or 2 more teaspoons of buttermilk or enough to make the dough cohesive. Let the dough rest, uncovered, for 5 or 6 minutes, until it is less sticky.

For each cracker, roll a generous ½ teaspoon of dough into a ball. Place the ball on a very well-greased or nonstick, spray-coated baking sheet. Cover with wax paper. Flatten each ball of dough into a 2-inch round with the bottom of a drinking glass, using a circular, rocking motion. Remove wax paper. Repeat until all the crackers are formed.

Bake the rounds for 8 to 11 minutes or until browned and crisp. Remove immediately from the baking sheet with a metal spatula. Cool on a wire rack. Store in an airtight container.

Makes 50 to 55 3-inch rounds

Index